remixing the ritual

hip hop theatre aesthetics

and practice

By Baba Israel

With a forward by Morganics

Remixing the Ritual: Hip Hop Theatre Aesthetics and Practice

Copyright © 2008 Baruch "Baba" Israel

Printed in the U.S.A.

Cover Painting by Yako

All rights reserved. No part of this book may be reproduced or transmitted in any form whatsoever, or by any means, electronic, or mechanical, including photocopying, or by any information storage or retrieval system, without permission in writing from the author.

Library of Congress Control Number: 2009903542

ISBN 978-0-578-01874-4

acknowledgements

Big up to the folks who supported this book, Boom Bap Meditations and my continued work in Hip Hop Theatre:

My wife and editor DawN Crandell, My foundation Steve and Pamela, Yako 440 (the music man), Morganics, Meta Bass 'n' Breath, Paul McIsaac, Akim Funk Buddah, Nomdaic Lotus, Core Rhythm, Playback NYC, Center for Playback Theater, Contact Theatre, The Living Theatre, Children's University Players, Bami (photography), Donna (Layout), Kwik Step and Roka (Full Circle), Universes, Kamilah Forbes, Clyde Vaentin, Danny Hoch, Hip Hop Theater Festival, Benji Reid, Breaking Cycles, My Goddard Advisors- Gale Jackson, Daniel Alexander Jones, Erica Eaton, Jackie Hayes and Bonnie Shock, The Goddard MFA IA community, Frisco (Sharpenin Swads), The Ford Foundation Future Aesthetics Regrant program, Jonzi D, Maxwell Golden, Martin Stanich, Rickerby Hinds, UCR, Daniel Banks, Hip Hop Theater Initiative, Claudia Alick, Oregon Shakespeare Festival, Willy Ney, First Wave Program, UWMadison, Michael Cirelli, Urban Word, Jaro Cossiga, Freaky Jesus, Nasty, Kuzhell, Dowis and Alesh one at Pantheon, Trinity International Hip Hop Festival, Philip, Sasha, and Maarten of Crime Jazz, Podium Mozaeik, Kai-Ti, Mike Supreme, Michael Fields, Dell Arte, David Bridell, New World Theater, Abrons Arts Center, 245 Live, Nicole Klaymoon, Teo Castellanos, Kevin Powell, Jlove, Jeff Chang and you for picking up this book!

table of contents

Forward 6
Artist Statement 7
Introduction 10
Continuity: Poem for my Parents 11
Hip Hop Theater: My Journey 13
The Elements of Hip Hop 15
Hip Hop's Origins 19
Revolutionary Rituals: Black arts 22
Minstrelsy VS Rap 25
Like a Signal Through the Flames: Born in the Theatre 32
Hip Hop Theatre: Reflections on the Work 36
Hip Hop Commedia: Facing the Mask 42
Hip Hop Theatre: Space and Place 45
Hip Hop Theatre: Aesthetic Articulation 51
Hip Hop's Aesthetic Voice 57
Hip Hop Theatre: Concerns, Contradictions, and Limitations 61
Hip Hop Theatre: The Future of the Remix 62
Boom Bap Meditations: Reflections on the Process 63
Script: Boom Bap Meditations 64
Building Blocks: The Path to Boom Bap Meditations 77
Process Journal: Creation of Boom Bap Meditations in Collaboration
    with Morganics 85
Multi-media/links 91
Bibliography 92
Performances 94
List of Plates 95

forward

Welcome to Baba-land. The book you have in your hand is the hard work, sweat, feelings, thoughts, meanderings, frustrations and celebrations of a guy who should be nominated for the hardest working man in Hip Hop. I have trailed through the streets, clubs, classrooms and theatres of New York in Baba's superhuman wake at a speed and rate that has at times left me looking like a sleepwalker. Wherever we go people stop him; old students on trains, theatre audiences catch him in restaurants, peers give him pounds and hugs outside clubs, crowds yell "Baba!!!" when he steps onstage and back in my homeland in Australia normally hardheaded MCs will take me aside in a late night club and say with a big smile on their face "How's that Baba fella going? I miss him."

This is one of the first books that is an accurate representation of a growing international form, Hip Hop Theatre. If you want to get an insight into where this form comes from, who are some of the artists involved, the politics and issues that it is concerned with, the cultural and historical context that it comes from or even the nitty gritty process of how a Hip Hop Theatre piece is made – check this out.

From countless all night New York street cyphers to Hip Hop Theatre pieces in backlane church halls in Sydney, from huge outdoor market concerts in Cambodia to smoke filled underground Hip Hop clubs in Prague, Baba has been putting it down. Performing, freestyling, connecting, teaching, learning, believing and ultimately in this book, sharing. Get an insight into this worldwide grassroots network that he is one of the pioneers of, hear of both his successes and failures, his joys and his pains and use it as bio fuel to give bloom to new thoughts, new questions, new directions, new work and more dope shit.

Enjoy, peace,
Morganics
July 2008

artist statement

As an **artist** I want to **tell** stories.
I want to tell my **story.**
I want to **hear** your **story** and **play it back**
through
improvisation and
theatre.

I was born into The Living Theatre, a tradition of art that challenged society and called out its oppressive forces. I continue in that tradition making music and theatre that address issues of race, militarization, and media manipulation.

hip hop

It is a culture that has shaped my voice and the way I move through the world.

I merge my love of Hip Hop and storytelling to take the stage and tell stories

through the characters i meet the verses i craft and the beats that back my flow

As a performer my background is in the Hip Hop and Spoken Word renaissance of the early nineties. Here my love of poetry, verses, and beats came to life alongside some of the greatest poets and emcees in the New York scene. As a child I was introduced to political theatre performing publicly in parks. After an invitation from Reg E. Gaines, I hit my first open mic at the Nuyorican Poets Cafe in 1993. Later, in the experimental scene of New York I performed improvisations in clubs, theatres, squats,

and raves. I collaborated with artists from diverse backgrounds including Hip Hop, Balinese dance, Jazz, Theatre of the Oppressed, Commedia dell'Arte and trained in Playback Theatre.

As an artist my school is not just the reading of books or the confines of conservatory. My skills have been crafted in street cyphers, late night wanderings, and my travels as performer and educator. As a playback conductor and performer I am reminded of the multitudes of stories and experiences that make up our world.

artist statement

My work in arts education is an integral part of my process. Through workshops and performances I interact with younger generations. I work with a range of communities, from kindergartners with expansive imaginations to high school students with attitude, real world struggles, and deep insight. These interactions keep me connected to current issues and trends.

The students I work with are inspiring and challenging. I experience first hand the destabilizing and limiting nature of popular culture. My philosophy as an educator is to facilitate a space that is inclusive of student's voice, struggles to be aware and critique oppressive paradigms while also nurturing creative discipline. I am interested in creating ensemble work that encourages group cooperation and support.

From within the popular form of Hip Hop I set out to learn and know its history, to critically engage its current manifestations, and to be part of envisioning new forms and innovations. As a student I find context and legacy in history. I decode artists, thinkers, and scholars who provide clues on my journey.

introduction

In the past as a solo artist I rocked Hip Hop shows and my theatrical work was ensemble based with Playback NYC. My first solo show *Boom Bap Meditations* came about as a result of the economic difficulties of ensemble work, facing my fears as a performer and a desire to push my creativity. I synthesized my skills as an emcee/poet/beatboxer/theatre artist in a new context of experimentation and learning.

Is *Boom Bap Meditations* performance art, solo theatre, or an example of Hip Hop Theatre? This book is an investigation full of questions about the implications, limitations and expansiveness of Hip Hop Theatre. In this book I place myself in conversation with theatre artists and Hip Hop artists to articulate a Hip Hop theatre aesthetic.

As a white man working and living in the culture of Hip Hop I must constantly and vigorously look at race. In America, we live in a system that is built on co-option and displacement. This displacement has roots in people, bodies, spirits and culture. American industry was literally built by displaced peoples. Our media is constantly displacing, replacing, and making invisible indigenous voices, voices of Black American culture, and the cultures of immigrants. In this book I explore the roots of race and performance in America from the racism of minstrelsy, the resistance of the Black Arts Movement, to the multicultural possibilities of Hip Hop.

continuity: poem for my parents

my parents
not your average   mom and dad
I never called them   mom and dad
they were   Pam and Steve

they were   not quite
your average parents
they gave me a home, good food, and tucked me in at night
as a kid they were more like
mentors sages

and sometimes bitter adversaries
they were wizards and sorceresses
giving me mad council
my father making tapes with me
trading stories and tales
my mother recording my dreams
telling me of goddess rituals

I remember watching my mother making masks
crocodiles, giant radioactive mutants, mythical creatures
surrounding my eyes

pops speaking sound sculptures with voice and word
weaving stories
making us all laugh with quick wit and deep heart

they were and are revolutionaries
who dreamt of another world
that isn't quite here yet

but they have never given up the struggle
the play and the vision
their craft their form
their creative fire has nurtured who I am today

hip hop theatre: my journey

hip hop

I was raised in the theatre and found my way to Hip Hop through the mobile gallery of graffiti and the late night mixes of Mr. Magic[1]. I found Hip Hop in the beatbox rhythms of my fifth grade classmate who swore he was Doug E. Fresh's[2] cousin. In 1985, I saw Hip Hop live and direct at the Beacon Theater with performances by Run-DMC, U.T.F.O., Roxanne Shante and The Real Roxanne. Hip Hop came downtown to West Broadway where B-Boys[3] got down on cardboard boxes. That same year I put my first rap on tape with SBG on the beatbox. I tried to scratch a Duran Duran record I had found and decorated with tags on a second hand record player. Then there were the late nights running through Soho with a spray can and a 40-ounce. Later came freestyle cypher[4], Rock Steady anniversaries, *All That* open mics, and countless shows, panels, and workshops.

There is a growing collection of Hip Hop documentation and more importantly living pioneers and practitioners who can break down Hip Hop and its history from a direct perspective. To set context I will offer an outline of Hip Hop's elements and origins. These are my thoughts in the context of my experience and learning. I encourage an open dialogue when attempting to define and state Hip Hop's aesthetic and story.

Hip Hop is an African diasporic cultural form born in the Bronx to Black and Latino parents with Afro-Caribbean grandparents. It has roots in the sound system culture of Jamaica, and the Blues, Rock, Jazz, Funk, and Disco of Black American music. Hip Hop is also influenced by European electronic music, martial arts films and culture, comic books, cartoons and other pop culture mythology. It is inherently a hybrid form with its foundation in the DJ mix where a wide range of musical styles and audio

---

[1] Host of WBLS radio show "Rap Attack" which debuted in 1983.
[2] One of the first prominent beatboxers.
[3] B-Boy or Break Boy- the Hip Hop cultural name for breakdancer.
[4] Freestyle Cipher- the art of improvised rhyme practiced in a circular formation featuring both collaboration and competitive verse.

sources are layered. Hip Hop contains the elements of dance (breaking, popping, and locking, as well as ever evolving social dances), music (DJing, beatboxing) poetry (emceeing), and visual art (graffiti).

In the Bronx of the seventies there was a climate of political corruption, gangs, arson, and a spark. This spark became DJs playing parties, dancers getting down to the beat, rappers dropping lyrics, and graffiti artists adding color and form to the walls. Hip Hop is interdisciplinary, it gives birth to self-motivated artists who master numerous forms. Hip Hop is a multi-track mix of contradictions. It is a form of cultural and political resistance nurturing an empowered voice for marginalized communities. Hip Hop is a dissonant DJ spinning a sound clash of patriarchal and homophobic content, affirmations of peace, social justice verses and violent materially obsessed lyrics. Hip Hop is at the cutting edge of technology, and as raw as spit and air. Hip Hop began in the Bronx, moved through the boroughs, the nation, and the world. Hip Hop is international; it has universal language and local specificity. The elements of Hip Hop each deserve their own book but to set context I will offer an outline of each.

the elements of hip hop

djs in Hip Hop have innovated the use of turntables as instruments. I grew up with the urban mythology of the turntable as the replacement for live instruments because of economic constraints. In *Making Beats: the Art of Sample Based Hip Hop* author Joseph G. Schloss challenges this notion with the assertion of the money required to refine and build both DJ gear and a record collection. "The idea that an individual could have access to a DJ system and thousands of obscure records, but not to more conventional musical instruments…is difficult to accept."[5] The DJ provided a new musical role. Instead of being limited to one instrument and depending on a band to get a big sound the DJ has the biggest and "baddest" bands at their fingertips. They manipulated the hits of the time, breaking new music in the context of the party. The DJ is the keeper of stories in the sense that they respond and guide the gathering with tunes that stimulate memory, evoke emotion, inspire love, motivate the party, and keep the peace.

[5] Schloss, Joseph Glenn. *Making Beats: The Art of Sample-Based Hip-Hop.* Middletown, CT: Wesleyan University Press, 2004. p. 29.

Hip Hop DJs such as Kool Herc used two copies of the same record to extend the break down or "break." This was the most percussive moment in the record that focused on the drums and the bass line. By using two turntables and a mixer the DJ had the ability to loop this break live by cutting back and forth. Grandmaster Flash added by using the DJ mixer and headphones to cue the next record allowing for greater accuracy. DJs such as Grand Wizard Theodore innovated the use of scratching, where the DJ places his hand directly on the vinyl isolating a short sound and then moving the record percussively to create new rhythms. This technique has evolved into turntablism[6] with DJs such as Qbert, Rob Swift, Mixmaster Mike, Roc Raida and DJ Kraze expanding the rhythmic complexity, use of DJ faders, and creating entire records and even films showcasing this art form.

breaking is an intricate combination of foot work, acrobatic power moves, poses and freezes that are driven by the break beat. Breaking has a rich choreographic language with traditional moves and a constantly expanding vocabulary. Breaking's roots are in an outlet of aggression and energy. In *Can't Stop Won't Stop* Jorge Pop Master Fabel Pabon says, "The style of a B-boy I never saw nothing like it. I'd never seen a dance approached like that original B-boy flavor, that straightforward, aggressive sort of I'ma-tear-up-this floor feeling."[7] Jeff Chang adds...

> The B-boys tapped into the same spirit that had given rise to New Orleans Mardi Gras Indian gangs...or Harlem's original Lindy Hoppers, the pioneering African-American jitterbuggers who emerged from pool hall gangs like the jolly fellows in the late 1920's to galvanize uptowns integrated nightclubs...with their floor steps, air steps and breakaways.[8]

In *Can't Stop Won't Stop Crazy Legs,* president of Rock Steady Crew, one of the longest running breaking crews, asserts that it wasn't Capoeira but James Brown who inspired their moves. Yet in Capoeira one sees a common language of resistance hidden in dance, of combat and code, and of turning the world upside down. I have always felt that Hip Hop is a primal and spiritual calling to ancient roots. There are very old and very human ways of relating and expressing that have been marginalized in

---

[6] Turntablism is a name coined by DJ Babu to describe the evolution of DJs as musicians.
[7] Chang, Jeff. *Can't Stop, Won't Stop: A History of the Hip-Hop Generation.* 1st ed. New York: St. Martin's Press, 2005. p. 115.
[8] Chang, Jeff. *Can't Stop, Won't Stop: A History of the Hip-Hop Generation.* 1st ed. New York: St. Martin's Press, 2005. p. 116.

our industrial and market driven culture. Hip Hop provides an almost tribal consciousness and community structure. I have felt this energy in the breaking circle. What is the language of breaking? Is it purely aggression, competition, bravado? Or is it also physical poetry, character, archetype? I see breaking as a language full of magic that challenges our perceptions of human limit and scientific law.

Popping and locking are two other Hip Hop dance forms. Locking comes out of Los Angeles, California and was invented by Don "Campbellock" Campbell. Locking is a dance based in the funk with wrist rolls, knee drops, and Uncle Sam points. In the seventies Popping was made famous by Boogaloo Sam and The Electric Boogaloos who were based in Fresno, California. It is a dance form that isolates muscle contractions in response to the beat. As a dance it can be robotic and precise or move fluidly. It has grown to include such styles as animation, ticking and "tutting" movements inspired by Egyptian imagery. Popping has roots in locking, the robot and mime techniques.[9]

emceeing is the poetic and lyrical expression of Hip Hop. Emceeing is also known as rapping but is distinguished by its skill set of crowd interaction, ceremonial mastery, and freestyle ability. Emceeing began as an addition to the party rocking of DJs with a focus on keeping the crowd hyped and engaged through call and response and lyrical routines. The art of the emcee evolved to the creation of original songs and albums with a diverse range of topics and styles. Emcees use poetic forms such as metaphor, simile, allusion and alliteration to craft rhymed verses.

beatboxing is the vocal interpretation of the drum machine or beat box. It was originally known as human beatboxing. Beatboxing has transformed into the vocal creation of multiple instruments. Beatboxers produce the sounds of drums, basses, guitars, horns, synthesizers, turntables, percussion, and intergalactic sound effects. Buff from the Fatboys, Doug E. Fresh, Ready Rock C, and Biz Markie are pioneers of the form. Beatboxing's second wave – Rahzel, Kenny Muhammad, and Scratch have inspired beatobxers, including me, to push the form even further. I am part of an active beatbox crew based in New York called Beatboxer Entertainment, founded by Kid Lucky.

---

[9] My information on Popping comes from direct interaction with Poppers such as Jazzy, Stretch Boogie, Pop Master Fabel, Mike Supreme, and B-boy Kwik Step.

graffiti is a visual form that predates but ultimately became an element of Hip Hop culture. Its roots are in gang culture and the neighborhood ritual of marking territory. First appearing in the late sixties, its visual style can range from "tags" which are the quick signatures of an artist. In the seventies full "productions" which are complex murals became popular. Graffiti's history is one of high risk and illegality, with a reward of "fame." Subway trains carried the artists' name throughout a city. The imagery of graffiti is linked to letter forms (wildstyle) and characters (comics, cartoons, Anime). Graffiti's intentions can run from the pure desire to "get up" or "get fame" or to honor lost ones, make political statements, or celebrate legends and heroes/sheroes.

hip hop*s origins

burnt history
bricks and buildings
White flight across
Cross Bronx Expressway
ghosts of Robert Moses
Hip Hop phoenix
from ashes of avarice
20th century plans to make projects with parks
parks that hold fear
soon bloom with beats

Why did Hip Hop begin in the Bronx? What was the climate of Hip Hop's origins? In *Can't Stop Won't Stop* author Jeff Chang reveals the history of industrial and real estate development in the Bronx by Robert Moses. With the building of the Cross Bronx expressway in 1953, came a route through the Bronx between the suburbs of New Jersey, Manhattan, and Queens. The expressway displaced large residential areas and Moses responded with plans for low-income housing that became the model for project housing. This residential shake up and suburban access contributed to the White exodus out of the Bronx.

In the seventies the Bronx was literally on fire. Slumlords used hired thugs to commit arson and collected big payouts off insurance money. Arson as profit is the complete corruption of capitalism. In the midst of this destruction Bronx youth gave birth to the life affirming and celebratory culture of Hip Hop. Hip Hop provided both a community outlet and alternative economic opportunity through the promoting of parties and street performance. Afrika Bambaataa transformed from Black Spade to founder of the Zulu Nation, moving from gang culture to positive organization. Hip Hop like any cultural movement is filled with contradictions and complexities. Hip Hop's individual artists and organized groups have both contributed to social transformation and propagated oppressive behaviors.

Jeff Chang writes "Neighborhood kids- many of them laughing, happy to be on television, no longer invisible- gathering to help firemen aim a hose at the threatening flames of the building next door."[10] In that moment of destruction, the youth of Bronx had the world's attention through the Bill Moyers CBS special *The Fire Next Door*. The image of the Bronx was one of lawlessness and destruction. The emergence of Hip Hop gave the Bronx a creative and expressive platform. Hip Hoppers were making media by creating tapes, flyers, and indie records.

Who are the storytellers of Hip Hop? Kool Herc described his parties as rights of passage. The DJ is a historian holding the collected stories of songs and improvising new combinations of song stories to create rituals of movement, celebration and honoring of the fallen. Emcees document alternative histories to the mainstream media and history books. Hip Hop created a cultural structure in the wake of destruction. The welcoming spirit of Hip Hop's pioneers heartens me.

afro-carribean grand parents

the language of dub
the version
endless and timeless echoplex
haunting reverb
hi hats beating down oppression
hidden meaning in chants
coded for rebel ears
love and angelic tones of seekers spirit voice
music potions concocted by sound alchemists mixing roots and riddims

Reggae's roots are in the foundations of Rhythm and Blues and the traditional African rhythms that survived slavery and colonialism. These roots birthed the original musical styles Ska, Rocksteady, Dub, and Dancehall. Political corruption and economic destabilization were present in the genesis of both Reggae and Hip Hop. In Jamaica thugs hired by conservative politicians attacked communities to shift votes. There were corporate pullouts after the rise of the socialist government. The CIA had a strong presence in government ploys to undermine Jamaica's *People's Party*.

---

[10] Chang, Jeff. *Can't Stop, Won't Stop: A History of the Hip-Hop Generation*. 1st ed. New York: St. Martin's Press, 2005. p. 16.

These actions echoed the destabilization of the Bronx and the undermining of Black and Latino political organizations. The borough of the Bronx was a microcosm of an island's cultural and political climate. It seems no coincidence that it would be a Jamaican (Kool Herc) who would give birth to Hip Hop. Reggae responded to Jamaica's political climate through rebel music, songs of rebellion and redemption. Hip Hop responded to institutionalized racism and economic corruption with a complex cultural movement that was fun, futuristic, and rebellious in its own right.

In *Cant Stop Wont Stop* Jeff Chang documents the rise of the sound system in Jamaica, describing it as a direct musical platform. The selectors in relation to their audience determined what music and culture flourished. This is a precursor for the independent media movement. Hip Hop and Reggae were born in block parties and yards. What does the rawness of these origins mean for Hip Hop today? Now many radio DJs are limited to a set playlist or replaced by a computerized system. DJs in the mainstream don't set trends or break new music; they simply affirm the dominant artists.

Hip Hop has become the greatest corporate advertising tool. Rap songs are filled with unpaid and unsolicited advertising where rappers run off brand names like Reggae artists quote biblical prophecy and conscious Hip Hop artists spit Black power language. Where can Hip Hop go? The rap industry is like a cultural slumlord. Now it is not the buildings that are burnt down but the artists. Record companies profit off the deaths and incarceration of rappers like slumlords collecting insurance money from arson. A burnt building is worth more than a functioning one; a dead or incarcerated rapper is worth more than a living one. We have lived with the unsolved murders of rappers Biggie Smalls and Tu-Pac and their constant post-mortem record releases. We also see it in the marketing of jailed artists such as rapper Shyne. Death, incarceration, and the criminalization of Rap music are celebrated in magazine articles, music videos and that mythology is exploited by the recording industry.

Is Rap's tongue corrupted by Babylon to the point of no redemption? Are the languages of Reggae and Hip Hop with their roots in religion, Rastafari, and the Five Percenters, a better alternative? Reggae's text is strong in Spirit but marred by patriarchy and homophobia. In the opposing absolutes of religious dogma and hyper materialism, where does a progressive voice birth in this Hip Hop language?

revolutionary rituals: black arts

In the deeply racist American paradigm our frameworks and references are linked to that racist lens. This effects the "when, why and how" of our conversation. Whose theatre? Whose music? Is it Shakespeare? Is it Elvis? In my early edits of this book many of my references were radical and experimental artists but they were also majority White and European. In looking at Hip Hop as an African diasporic form and a Black aesthetic we must learn and engage Black Arts traditions when discussing a Hip Hop Theatre aesthetic.

In the introduction of *The Theatre of Black Americans: Roots and Rituals* Errol Hill sets the context for Black American Theatre. He illustrates its role in social and political process and specifically in its function to struggle against racism and assert a redefined Black identity. He also illuminates the role of Black Theatre in reclamation of community ritual both in connection to African tradition/religious rites and the creation of modern secular community ritual.

In the essay *Two Afro-American Contributions to Dramatic Form* Eleanor W. Traylor offers, "First of all, all that can be called representative American Theatre is Afra-American."[11] Traylor situates that the African traditions of song, dance, mask, and ritual brought to America through slavery are woven into American theatrical history. She also broadens my understanding of minstrelsy revealing its pre-White roots as a "masking" ritual. I assumed minstrelsy was a racist practice of Whites donning Black face and the mockery of Black stereotypes. Traylor continues,

> *What White performers spied down field, up field, or around the slave cabins was a masking performance.... They borrowed the "illusion", severing that from the reality that shaped it.... They observed a theatrical form which in essence was choral and*

---

[11] Traylor, W. Elanor "Two Afro-American Contributions to Dramatic Form" The Theater of Black Americans: A Collection of Critical Essays. Ed. Hill, Errol. Englewood Cliffs, N.J: Prentice-Hall, 1980. Pg. 47.

> *improvisational. Many sacred and secular Afro-American forms contained the choric improvisational call-and-response motifs.*[12]

It would follow then, that the function of these early rituals was taken out of context and transformed by the racist White paradigm. This transformation of masking rituals into what we know as minstrelsy sets the stage for a constant White redefinition of Black Theatre and performance. The minstrel tradition became a major influence on the mainstream musical theatre form that America made famous.

Choric improvisation and call-and-response are vital elements of Black aesthetics. These elements travel through time from the church, Blues, Jazz, Funk to the emcee and DJ creating a community ritual in Hip Hop. As the emcee leads the audience in a chant or asks is "Brooklyn in the house?" They are part of a legacy of affirming connection in a displaced and disconnected reality. That collaborative, communal and ritualistic approach marks a distinct tradition vital to the emergence of Hip Hop Theatre.

The arrival of the twentieth century brought new immigrant communities and a rise in European theatre forms. White America continued its legacy of co-opting Black forms from the Blues, Rock and Roll, to eventually Hip Hop. This co-option leads to a rewriting of history. We see this in the cultural placement of Rock and Roll as an often-perceived White form. There is a constant struggle between the transformation of Black aesthetics into White validated forms and the institutional elitism of European aesthetics. Black Theatre creates its own identity in both content and form in relation to dominant European theatre aesthetics.

> *Central to the debate over the function and structure of Black theatre, then as, it's the prevailing view that the theatre of Black Americans should by definition be distinct from that of White America. The two societies identified by the federal government's 1968 Kerner Report, have through their widely contrasting experiences, arrived at different conceptions of reality that seem to demand different modes of expression. Black theatre that appears to be analogous in form to the established Euro-American Theatre is therefore deemed to be a thoughtless imitation of an alien culture and a betrayal of the true heritage of the race.* [13]

---

[12] Traylor, W. Elanor "Two Afro-American Contributions to Dramatic Form" *The Theater of Black Americans: A Collection of Critical Essays*. Ed. Hill, Errol. Englewood Cliffs, N.J: Prentice-Hall, 1980. Pg. 49.

[13] Hill, Errol. *The Theater of Black Americans: A Collection of Critical Essays*. Englewood Cliffs, N.J: Prentice-Hall, 1980. p. 5.

The Civil Rights era had moments of successful alliances across the color line but those alliances faced continued hate crimes and overt violent racism. In a landscape of race riots, the assassinations of leaders such as Malcolm X and Martin Luther King Jr., emerged both the nationalism and self-determination of the Black Power Movement and its cultural sibling the Black Arts Movement. As the Black Power Movement developed and refined Black organizing, the Black Arts Movement created radical and controversial artistic structures that directly attacked White America with cutting, defined, and violent imagery. The theatre that came out of this movement challenged traditional Black roles and western structures. Within the Black Arts Movement came a rigorous denial of European form and a reclamation of Black aesthetics.

Amiri Baraka, an initiator of the Black Arts Movement, reflected a merging of verse and music. His work unites the senses in the magic of text and tone. The rhythms of his words and the musical delivery deepen the transmission.

> *The use of music must be understood. Music goes more deeply into the spirit than words; music is a living creature, a human intellectual and emotional creation with a readily apparent spirituality that transcends the visible world of its creators. It goes out of the world. It is not bound by our physicality. The sounds carry whatever information rests in the frequencies and rhythms and harmonies of the world, some known to us, some unknown.*[14]

Here Baraka reveals the transcendental nature of the Black aesthetic. The work can deal with the present day and material world but through the music it is connected to an ancestral and universal continuum. The layers of movement, music and verse in relation to a legacy of ritual allow for a deep investigation and revelation. The music is not simply to entertain but is a medium of spirit. This spirit is conducted in the modern rituals of the New Black Theatre. Shelby Steele writes.

> *One of the most salient characteristics of the New Black Theatre that maintains its separation from mainstream American drama is its ritualistic aspect. By ritualistic, I mean the strong presence of symbols, characterizations, themes and language styles which are frequently repeated from play to play and over a period of*

---

[14] Baraka, Amiri "Bopera Theory" *Black Theatre: Ritual Performance in the African Diaspora* Ed. Harrison, Paul Carter, Victor Leo Walker, and Gus II. Edwards.. Philadelphia: Temple University Press, 2002. p. 379.

> *time, with the result that easily recognized patters are established which have the function of reaffirming the values and particular commitment of the audience for whom the plays are written.*[15]

This ritualistic intentionality connects to the rituals of Africa and of survival in the dehumanizing structure of slavery. The New Black Theatre was part of navigating the chaos and possibility of twentieth-century America. Steele describes a theatre that challenges western notions of "arts for arts sake" and builds an aesthetic married to political content. This theatre created a multi-sensory language to resist oppressive forces and redefine the Black identity. The works were not individual but rather the theatre was a part of a larger social, spiritual and political process.

The New Black Theatre marked a celebration of Black language and marked a code for differentiation between outsider and insider. Steele references the tradition in theatre of language as a marker of class and extends that concept to illustrate the use of Black slang, hip talk, and vernacular as a tool that confuses/separates White audiences. This "overt" secret language resonates with the ever changing slang of Hip Hop. The accessibility, commercialization, and cross-cultural use of slang raise questions of its ability to remain a political/cultural tool.

Reading *Notes on Ritual in the New Black Theatre* by Shelby Steele I was struck by the militant, nationalistic, and separatist content and structures in the theatrical work of the New Black Theatre. The role of White people in many of the plays coming out of the Black Arts Movement were intentionally reduced to characterizations. These characterizations reinforced either the White female seductress whose "innocence" endangered the Black men she targeted, or the transformation of the White man into a homosexual desiring the Black man. The disturbing trends of homophobia and anti-Semitism were explicitly part of the structures Steele describes. It is important to situate those structures in relation to the hundreds of years of White domination and exploitation and specifically of the violent oppressiveness of Black portrayal in American performance and the racist limitations imposed on Black performers.

Hip Hop as a cultural form has not been as explicit or militant in its self-identification as a Black aesthetic in the same way as the Black Arts Movement. Although X-Clan, Public Enemy, and Poor Righteous Teachers

---

[15] Steele, Shelby "Ritual in the New Black Theater" *The Theater of Black Americans: A Collection of Critical Essays*. Ed. Hill, Errol. Englewood Cliffs, N.J: Prentice-Hall, 1980. p. 30.

reflect a Black nationalistic identity, Hip Hop also has an inclusive and global intention represented by artists KRS-One and Afrika Bambaataa. Bambaataa's legendary record Planet Rock embodies his musical and cultural mission to promote Hip Hop as a uniting force. His creation of the Universal Zulu Nation with members from not only the Bronx but across Europe, Africa, Australia and Asia represents his global vision for Hip Hop. KRS One, as an emcee has consistently addressed political and social issues vital to the Black community but also situated himself as a humanist. His projects such as H.E.A.L. (Human Education Against Lies) and the Temple of Hip Hop present platforms that are not solely race specific.

In the early nineties the lyrical content of the Hip Hop and Spoken Word scenes echoed the Black Arts Movement. "White devil lyrics" were a staple in the emcee's or poet's taking on the White oppressor. I came up as an artist in that time and while I find such attitudes around race ultimately limiting it was an important layer in the continual facing of my own racism and privilege. If artists do not take strong and unwavering stances it is hard to counteract the dominant paradigms. I wonder if Hip Hop's multiplicity and current multi-cultural make up might allow for new dialogue? Unfortunately I have seen many Hip Hop venues become Whiter and Whiter creating a new kind of detached superiority and manipulation of Black aesthetics. To counteract that, as a White artist involved in the creation of Hip Hop and Hip Hop Theatre it is essential that I directly interact with a diverse range of Black practitioners and audience.

minstrelsy vs rap

There is a continuum in the Black aesthetic, a language, spirit, ritual, and form that moves through the minds, voices, and bodies of Black artists. The deftness of word, power of cadence, and mastery of ritual moves through the pastor, bluesman, poet and emcee.

There is another continuum, that of the continued cooption and transformation by White America of the Black Aesthetic. In the marketing of Hip Hop (Rap music) Blackness is played out in exaggerations of ignorance, hyper sexuality and violence. The stereotypes of minstrelsy created characters who transform contextually but consistently find root in our American consciousness.

In much of early mass media Blackness was either invisible, or relegated to the minstrel roles. In the current popular culture I see minstrelsy's offspring everyday on MTV and BET. How is it that after Civil Rights, the Black Arts Movement and Hip Hop, we have come back to these stereotypes?

In the essay *Black Face and Blackness: The Minstrel Show in American Culture* Eric Lott explores the role of minstrelsy as both a racist practice and an example of authentic American art and culture. Here once again we experience the layers of authentic Black expression and a White manipulated form. The early "masking rituals" where slaves negotiated their social experience through parody and burlesque were transformed into the racist "Black face" minstrel form.

Mark Twain extolling the cultural impact of minstrelsy feels like the same racist and condescending praise given to movies like *Hustle and Flow* by White people today. *Hustle and Flow* is a film that tells the story of a Black pimp turned rapper. It is a film made by a White man and portrays misogynistic and sexist content in the context of a "Hustla" getting local acclaim. Eric Lott writes.

> ...James Weldon Johnson similarly remarked that minstrelsy... constituted the only "completely original contribution" of America to the Theatre.... These judgments appear terribly mis-

> *guided now, given that Black face minstrelsy's century long commercial regulation of Black cultural practices stalled the development of African-American public arts and generated an enduring narrative of racist ideology.*[16]

How do we negotiate the authentic artistic contributions of minstrelsy origins and also challenge its racist and limiting legacy? In our current mainstream popular culture, race is being played to the extreme. This extremity is witnessed in the images of southern rap music videos, rapper 50 Cent, films like *Hustle and Flow* and VH1's the *White Rapper Show*. Here we once again see the development and support of a range of creative voices being stalled in lieu of a continued racist narrative. I am also concerned that radical Black and multi-racial arts movements have been erased from popular public consciousness.

In the essay *Social Commentary in White Minstrelsy*, Robert C. Toll discusses the role of minstrelsy in commenting on society. This commentary had its foundation in the assertion of Black inferiority as a method of maintaining White supremacist mythology. In post Civil War America it also took on the rising women's movement as a threat to White males social position. In addition the White minstrel form expanded to take on immigrant groups, creating caricatures by amplifying physical and cultural characteristics such as food, language and music. We still see this today. Earlier I asked why are these images returning, but that isn't the right question. Why have these images never left our consciousness? Racism is deeply rooted in all of our minds and its mythology is maintained not just by legal and political systems but also by our cultural vision.

Toll asserts that this White minstrelsy served as way for audiences to comprehend the major social upheavals of post-slavery, women's rights, and the shifting population of immigrants. The disturbing code for me is the assumed default audience of White men. The assertion of these stereotypical characters served only the needs of White men. We still feel this default audience perspective informing much of our current media. There have been countless struggles of oppressed people to challenge and humanize representation of women, people of color, and immigrants in the media and arts. During the late eighteen hundreds the only groups that seemed to move forward were the Irish and Germans who moved

---

[16] Lott, Eric "Black Face and Blackness: The Minstrel Show in American Culture" Ed. *Inside the Minstrel Mask: Readings in Nineteenth-Century Blackface Minstrelsy*. Bean, Annemarie. Hatch, James Vernon, and Brooks McNamara. Hanover, NH: Wesleyan University Press, 1996. p. 5.

from positions of ridicule to a broader human representation. I see this directly connecting with the movement of European immigrants into the group of "Whiteness."

Even as topics in these minstrel shows moved from representations of Blackness, Black face was still used and spoken dialect became the marker of race. Toll describes Black face as a tool to make the social commentary palatable in the way the fool of Europe functioned. The perversion here is that this fool represented an entire race as opposed to an amplified character.

In reading this history, the lineage of American sketch comedy becomes very clear. Black and now Latino performers have moved into this tradition to not only critically examine their own communities but also challenge White racism. Comedians such as the Wayans Brothers, Dave Chappelle, and Carlos Mencia have all played with stereotypes to create social commentary. In Toll's essay he also describes White minstrelsy's target both Chinese and Japanese communities. They were marked as exotic, untrustworthy, and dangerous. Their alienation from mainstream society was reinforced. This tradition is alive in our current media and has expanded to focus on people of Arabic descent in reaction to the "War on Terror." I have not seen sketch comedy coming out of the Asian community but comedians like Margaret Cho have used stereotype to address the cultural and political concerns of her community.

The Hop of Fashion (c. 1856) by Charles T. White, tells the story of a Black man winning the lottery and throwing a ball and not knowing the social codes. This story reminds me of the MTV reality show *Adventures in Hollyhood*. This show features Memphis group Three 6 Mafia living in a mansion with their assistants. It is a bizarre clash of country/hood culture and Hollywood high class. There is a similar kind of mockery and exploitation of these performers. Do they have a choice in how they are portrayed? Do we live in a time where there are other choices? Whose idea was it for this show? Who writes and plans it? It is in the tradition of minstrelsy in that *Adventures in Hollyhood* shows us heightened stereotypes of Blackness in the context of the White world of Hollywood executives, blonde actresses, and plays at their ignorance and folly in navigating that world.

The shifting of America's and ultimately the world's popular imagination concerns me. At Hip Hop's creative and political height there were strong artistic representations of Blackness that blasted thru cable TV and on to the big screen. Slowly but surely that has shifted to the "shuckin and jivin" of much of Rap. How did this shift occur? Was it a political decision made in a closed meeting, was the FBI involved? Were there payoffs, industry deals or shakedowns? Was there an organic shift in collective consciousness? Or is it just more entertainment for White folks?

In the essay *Cycles of Transgression from Cool White to Vanilla Ice* by W.T. Lhamon, Jr. the author posits that minstrelsy played a similar role to Rock 'n' Roll and Hip Hop in the lives of young Whites. He describes it as a release and way to challenge the moral codes of the established apprentice system.

> *Youths were of course no more accepting of external control in the nineteenth century then they are in the late twentieth. As now, youths worried then about how to represent their overwhelming social forces to themselves. The minstrel show was their form countering the channeling merchants imposed.*[17]

I struggle with this analysis not because it isn't true but because it lacks a critical racial perspective. It assumes youth to be White and the dominant force seeking refuge in the margins of the Black experience and in this case an imitated Black experience. As a White youth I also sought refuge from the repressive structure of Whiteness within Black culture. A major difference is; the Black culture I encountered, unlike the minstrel show was for the most part Black created. This balance of power shifted with the rise of corporate involvement in the rap industry. Now, there is a similar relationship to the one he describes in the current Hip Hop or Rap world. Whites imitate and fetishize gangster rap, pimp, and playa stereotypes. Escaping the moral coding of dominant White religious values in the stereotypes of Black culture, Whites create a pattern of reinforcing negative behavior as a form of rebellion. This is where privilege comes in- for Whites this exploration/rebellion is transitory and often limited to youth. The negative social and institutional ramifications of racism for Black youth are a life long experience.

> *The minstrel show was the first among many later manifestations, nearly always allied with images of Black culture, that*

---

[17] Lhamon Jr., W.T. "Cycles of Transgression from cool White to Vanilla Ice" *Inside the Minstrel Mask: Readings in Nineteenth-Century Blackface Minstrelsy*. Ed. Bean, Annemarie. Hatch, James Vernon, and Brooks McNamara. Hanover, NH: Wesleyan University Press, 1996. *p. 277.*

> *allowed youths to resist merchant defined external impostures...White youths in the 1830s were shaping the minstrel show as a way of resisting merchant control. Abstracting themselves as Blacks allowed their heterogeneous parts all access to the same identification.*[18]

This makes me think of the young White record executives, members of the White Hip Hop press, and White media purchasers who play a role in maintaining the stereotypes of Black culture. When I read this article I really crave to hear a Black voice in this context. The Black experience is consistently marginalized and explored through a White context. What did minstrelsy mean for Black youth? Who set moral and social codes for Black youth? Where did Black youth find their rebellion and freedom? Were there radical Whites that were challenging the stereotypes of minstrelsy?

In minstrelsy and its transformation from "masking" ritual to racist propaganda a cycle is revealed, a cycle of White co-option of Black forms and redistribution in new rituals that affirm America's racist legacy. I see the transformation of this cycle adding the layer of class creating a complex multi-racial conspiracy to propagate and support limiting, oppressive, and stereotypical content into the mass consciousness. I bear witness to a legacy of Black, Indigenous, White and with new movements of immigration since slavery a broader "People of color", who constantly struggle to challenge and break this agenda. In the Black Arts Movement there was strong and direct action to shatter the racist legacies of White manipulation and dominance. I crave the development and support of well rounded and layered artists who represent the complexity of the human experience. It is my hope that the current multi-racial Hip Hop culture and its movement into theatre will provide a new and vigorous space of creative resistance.

---

[18] Lhamon Jr., W.T. "Cycles of Transgression from cool White to Vanilla Ice" *Inside the Minstrel Mask: Readings in Nineteenth-Century Blackface Minstrelsy*.Ed. Bean, Annemarie. Hatch, James Vernon, and Brooks McNamara. Hanover, NH: Wesleyan University Press, 1996. *p. 278.*

like a signal through the flames: born in the theatre

My history in theatre is one of direct experience, of family, frustration and excitement. I was not trained in a conservatory; my study of theatre has been far from traditional. I want to interrogate assumptions of tradition and legitimacy. I see Hip Hop and its convergence with theatre in a continuum of asserting marginalized traditions. I also see this in the continuum of Black aesthetics and radical multi-racial theatre movements.

As a theatre artist a great deal of my experience is from my work with Playback NYC, an improvisational ensemble that I co-founded with Paul McIsaac.

Formed in New York City in 1998, Playback NYC performs in theatres, clubs, schools, prisons, with unions and other community groups. Our Playback work is informed by the foundation created by Jonathan Fox and Jo Salas in 1975, and by our interaction with the international Playback Theatre community.

Playback is a theatrical form that focuses on the citizen as actor. It breaks down the separation between audience and performer by creating an interactive ritual. In a Playback performance the audience is invited by the conductor to share feelings and thoughts, which are transformed into short form improvisations by the actors and accompanying musician. This prepares the audience for the telling of a longer story where an audience member takes the teller's chair to share a longer story. The feelings and stories of a gathered audience shape a larger story weaving what in Playback is known as the "red thread." Playback's foundation is in the ancient ritual of community storytelling. The priority is not a single artist's vision but a collective artistic process that honors the community's direct stories. Playback's power is its universal relevance. A Playback company does not bring a piece of theatre that assumes it is relevant to a given community, rather it creates a theatre based on that community's

Playback NYC uses music, dance, freestyle Hip Hop and improvisation to transform the stories of our audience into the art of theatre. Rooted in ancient story telling traditions and tempered by current poetic and musical forms, we take our script from our audiences; memories, feelings, dreams, social and political conflicts are all transformed into theatre by our actors and musicians.

story and experience. This requires a deep commitment to honoring each interaction, and is aided by a group that carries a rich diversity. In our Playback company we have a commitment to racial, gender, sexuality, age, and class diversity. As a Playback conductor and performer I have heard and played back stories I would never hear in the movements of my own life. This is a privilege, as a Playbacker my views of the world are directly expanded each time we perform.

Our ensemble has also developed its own variations on Playback forms through extensive rehearsal and performance experimentation. In the improvisation we strive to find metaphorical representations of our audience's input as opposed to melodramatic forms. Playback has developed my ability as an improviser and an ensemble player as well as fostered an approach of collective creation and a community based focus and intention. Our company has also presented an improvisational/scripted piece *What You Say White Boy?* The piece fuses Hip Hop with the comedy of traditional Commedia dell'Arte.

I grew up in the Living Theatre. Mine was a childhood of theatre, rehearsal spaces, loft parties, and passionate conversations. The Living Theatre, established in 1947 by Judith Malina and Julian Beck, carries a vital theatrical history with a commitment to public, political, and collective development. Their early works such as The Brig confronted the brutality of military prisons and *The Connection* explored the world of Jazz. The Living Theatre left America and toured Europe throughout the sixties and seventies. Their work marked essential developments in street theatre and collective creation. In Europe works such as *Paradise Now* and *Mysteries and Smaller Pieces* moved from traditional theatrical forms to ritualistic and improvisational structures. Their theatre moved from the stage into the audience and spilled into the streets. The company traveled to Morocco, was jailed in Brazil, and retuned to America creating site-specific works such as the *Money Tower*, which dealt with class structure and was performed in front of steel mills in Pittsburg, Pennsylvania. After extensive European touring, in 2007 they returned to New York City to open a theatre and remount *The Brig*.

When I was ten years old I was a member of a youth theatre company, run by Gypsy, a member of The Living Theatre. This was an important introduction to theatre and performance. We created anti-consumerism plays and I played Ronald "Raygun" performing in public parks around New York City. The work was political and public, which has been an important thru line in my work.

After leaving that company I found so much of the theatre I saw to be condescending, dull, irrelevant to my experience, and in Hip Hop terminology "wack." In reading Ntozake Shange's essay *unrecovered losses/Black theatre traditions* I found a critique that situates some of my own frustrations. She writes "As a poet in American theatre I find most activity that takes place on our stages overwhelmingly shallow/stilted and imitative. That is probably one of the reasons I insist on calling myself a poet or writer rather than a playwright."[19] I feel that the poets and emcees of the Hip Hop generation are redefining the possibilities of performance and theatre.

In my early twenties I lived in Sydney, Australia. There I met and worked with Morgan Lewis (Morganics), a seasoned Hip Hop and theatre performer. Until this meeting I saw the worlds of Hip Hop and theatre as separate. I was excited and invigorated with the thought of their collision and connection. Morganics has been an inspiration for me;

---

[19] Shange, Ntozake. *Three Pieces*. 1st pbk. ed. New York: St. Martin's Press, 1992. p. 4.

his solo performance and our collaborations have helped to shape my artistic process. Morganics's background in experimental performance and Hip Hop has shaped him into an artist that continually challenges traditional theatre aesthetics. His work is often non-linear, physical, and pulls from Hip Hop's aesthetic of sampling, looping, and layering. He works with found text, tight transitions, repetition, and rhythmic sensibility. His latest solo show *Crouching B-Boy, Hidden Dreadlocks* also pushes the emotional range of Hip Hop Theatre digging deep into the personal effects of prison and poverty.

hip hop theatre: reflections on the work

Enter Hip Hop Theatre, a recipe for my excitement and engagement in the theatrical tradition. Hip Hop Theatre is a work in progress. It is a young form full of energy and possibility. I want to reflect on the early work that I have experienced. These reflections plant the seed for an articulation of a Hip Hop Theatre aesthetic. Hip Hop Theatre expands Hip Hop's ability to tell stories allowing for a greater range of content, emotion, and dynamic outside of the hype of the club/party. Yet when Hip Hop moves into the theatre does it lose its rawness? I see this tension as a vital place to examine the development of the form.

It is important to note that Hip Hop Theatre has an international history with, to my knowledge, groups and projects forming in the United States, U.K., Holland, and Australia. I also want to locate my initiation within Hip Hop Theatre within my work in Australia with Morganics and my experiments with Akim the Funk Buddha and the Nomadic Lotus Collective in NYC. Akim is a performing artist whose work explores urban and indigenous connections. He is from Zimbabwe, Africa and infuses his theatrical performance with diverse forms such as beatboxing, emceeing, breaking, popping, Balinese movement, and Tuuvan throat singing to make connections across cultures. I worked with Akim from 1994–1998. We created art that broke open my expectations of improvisational performance. We challenged notions of traditional venue, creating spontaneous and interactive experiences in restaurants, street corners, trains, raves, ashrams, and university hallways. Sometimes we met a person on the way to the "show" at a theatre and they would end up in the piece. The lines between off and on stage blurred with our lives.

In 1996, in Australia I worked on a Hip Hop Theatre piece called *The Bridge*. We had a DJ providing the soundtrack and used graffiti as our set and backdrop. The piece told the story of Enzyme, a character that moved through the elements of Hip Hop while facing the challenges of family life, the police, school and ultimately self. The show began with the audience gathered outside a school hall. The actors began as a group of students who decided to break into the hall urging the audience to follow. Inside the hall there were four stages with action also moving into the center. The audience did not sit but rather moved around the space observing and sometimes interacting with the different scenes. We successfully merged the movement and spontaneity of Hip Hop with the range that theater allows. The audience could cheer and interact with emcees or witness the private and vulnerable moment of a family. This was my initiation and set a foundation for my instincts, techniques, and questions in devising, performing, and directing Hip Hop Theatre.

In terms of seeing and experiencing work in the States, the Hip Hop Theatre Festival is a primary supporter of the form. I also acknowledge *Jam on the Groove*[20] as a starting point of Hip Hop Theatre. Daniel Banks has also been a consistent supporter of Hip Hop Theatre helping to give it life in the academic context and breaking new ground with the Hip Hop Theatre initiative. The First Wave program at the University of Madison is another university based program encouraging the development of the form. Benji Reids *Process Festival* is at the forefront of Hip Hop Theatre training creating a laboratory environment that supports skill building and innovation. I appreciate Benji's commitment to not only producing work but also producing a festival that nurtures the genre and promotes the next generation of Hip Hop Theatre. There are many great artists whose work I have not yet reflected on such as Willpower, Benji Reid, Ben Snyder, and Rha Goddess. I hope to look at these and other artists in future revisions.

At the Nuyorican Poets Café in 1999, and again at the Hip Hop Theatre Festival in 2001, I saw *Rhyme Deferred* directed by good friend Kamilah Forbes. This was an important piece for me in that it broke open a lot of my own expectations and thoughts around Hip Hop Theatre. I was exited and moved to see emceeing, DJing, and breaking fused with theatre. The piece had all the energy of a Hip Hop show. Its aesthetic was Hip Hop; there were well-crafted verses, delectable DJ cuts, fierce breaking, and dope beats.

Though I had worked on *The Bridge* this was my first time as a member of the audience experiencing Hip Hop Theatre. The Hip Hop elements of the show were executed with skill, the politics were on point, and yet some how I wasn't completely engaged. I was used to feeling and evaluating a

---

[20] Ghetto Originals Hip Hop Dance Theater show.

Hip Hop record or a live show— but a Hip Hop Theatre piece— this was new territory. It wasn't just about the rhyme styles or skills of the dancers or the quality of the beats. There were new elements to consider. I talked with friend and mentor Paul McIsaac and he commented on the show's rhetorical nature.

The piece was based on Cain and Able and on the struggle between the mainstream and underground worlds of Hip Hop. In the piece *Rhyme Deferred* there existed a static and binary definition of good and evil, of just and unjust, and of righteous and wicked. This led to a language and mode that caused the poetry and lyricism to border on rhetoric. I have come to realize that theatre offers an opportunity to explore complex contradictions, layers, and rounded edges.

In conversation with Kamilah[21] she reflected on the timing of the work. When *Rhyme Deferred* was created it was a time of major transition in Hip Hop and the piece reflected a reaction to that transition. It was the rise of Bad Boy Records, hyper- materialism, violence, and sexuality. When I look at my own writing from that time, these issues were also a central theme. Kamilah also shared that *Ryhme Deferred* contained the layers of spirit and ritual. This connects her to the legacy of the Black Arts Movement and to her later work on Scourge. I value Kamilah's commitment as an artist and her support of Hip Hop Theatre's development. Her latest work *Scourge* exhibits artistic maturity, thought it does not have the obvious Hip Hop characters and elements in full display it invokes a layered ritual that is certainly driven by the Hip Hop aesthetic.

I went to see *Scourge*, an ensemble work directed by Kamilah Forbes and written by Marc Bamuthi Joseph on June 8th 2007. The fusion of language and music was Hip Hop. There were moments where the poetry felt like a DJ cutting in and out of the beat. This poetry was performed in unison voice and the accompanying physicality heightened the sense of rhythm and musical connection. The music in the piece had a strong Hip Hop aesthetic. It combined elements of funk, soul, beatbox, and Afro-Caribbean rhythms and song. There were moments of rhyme and emceeing that were integrated into the storytelling and moved with personality and clarity. The music supported and enhanced the poetic performance.

Scourge confronted notions and fears about voodoo and African diasporic spirituality. The themes of the performance focused on Haiti's history and

---

[21] Conversation with Kamilah Forbes on Nov 10th 2007.

current struggles. It also raises issues facing Haitian immigrant communities in the United States. At its heart the piece was a ritual and therefore the traditional theatre space felt limiting. I am curious what the piece might feel like in another space. The action wanted to expand beyond the stage's borders.

In the Hip Hop Theatre movement Jonzi D, an artist from England, moves me. He is a skilled emcee, poet, theatre performer, and dancer. He also weaves his own cultural language, slang, and political context into his performance. His work is edgy and full of love; confronts the audience, and also confronts himself.

In his piece *Lyrical Fearta* he plays with moments of temptation. He evokes scenarios where he shows the range of his character. He explores moments of lust and violence and then uses movement and music (DJ scratching) to transcend them. He takes the audience to the edge of an action and uses movement to bring to life the complexity of dealing with the human experience.

In *Shoota*, Jonzi explores violence in a direct way. His body language, walk, and tone shift as a gun is brandished and ultimately aimed at the audience. He directly confronts the audience members. Challenging our fears of violence, and for some our fears of Black men with guns. He doesn't talk about violence or guns or fear, he becomes the catalyst and agent to demand our comprehension. We don't think, "Oh violence is wrong," we don't think "Oh we should not fear Black men;" no we are brought to the edge of those moments and allowed to process them on our own. Jonzi then, in a violent and sexualized climax masturbates the gun in a final ejaculatory explosion where there is not life but death.

In Antoin Artaud's *Theatre and its Double* Artuad talks about the creation of a Theatre of Cruelty- he describes a theatre unlike the classical theatrical relationship where the audience is a passive. Artaud writes "I suggest a theatre today ought to return to the fundamental magic notion reintroduced by psychoanalysis, which consists in curing a patient by making him assume the external attitude of the desired location."[22]

This quote highlights for me what Jonzi accomplishes in his work. I am engaged, I am not a passive voyeur but a participant whose interaction is both invited and demanded. This is a central element of Hip Hop and for me an essential element of Hip Hop Theatre. In my work as an artist I

---

[22] Artaud, Antonin. *The Theater and its Double*. New York: Grove Press, 1958. p. 80.

have always been interactive, but in my musical life I have found my interaction to be based around joyous call and response, the uplifting tradition of positive affirmation and celebration. In my theatrical life I need to expand my interactive possibilities. It is a scary and exciting place to work from. The creation of a Theatre of Cruelty at first seems contradictory to my artistic direction but as I read and explore I find that it might be a vital and necessary ingredient in the creative process of my work.

One of the challenges of Hip Hop Theatre is in its desire to be an alternative from the violence, sexism, misogyny, and homophobia of mainstream rap it can become to nice, clean, and politically correct. In order to deal with the core issues that create our human ills we have to exorcise them. By invoking and exploring these ills in the realm of theatre, they can be challenged, made fun of or defeated.

Danny Hoch is another integral member of the Hip Hop Theatre movement. As performer, writer, director and organizer he has contributed artistically and structurally to the development of this work. His piece *Jails, Hospitals, and Hip Hop* is a brilliant solo show. I remember journeying into a multitude of worlds and important issues through his characters.

I went to see Danny Hoch's play *Till the Break of Dawn* in previews on September 4th, 2007. I will focus on the question does this piece represent a push forward in the creation of Hip Hop Theatre? More specifically does it create a Hip Hop Theatre aesthetic? Danny Hoch's view on Hip Hop Theatre has been that it is more related to content then form. There were emcees in the play but we never heard any lyrics or poetry. Music was relegated to black out transitions. The cultural references, slang, and fashion of Hip Hop were present but I felt an absence of theatrical action and specifically the heightened possibilities of movement, poetics, and the musicality of Hip Hop's aesthetics. Were there issues and ideas that I found relevant? Yes. Was the writing strong with important questions and content? Yes. Yet I was left wishing to experience the energy of Hip Hop, live and direct.

I recently saw an excerpt of Danny Hoch's new piece *Taking Over* which deals with gentrification in Williamsburg, Brooklyn. The monologue was spot on, balancing humor and the oppressive reality of the current culture clash on BK streets. I can't wait to see this show and I am excited for Danny's take on this issue, which hits home to me as a native New Yorker.

In 2007, I went to Miami to experience the Miami Hip Hop Project which featured performances of *The Sixth Vowel* by Nicole Klaymoon and Rudi

Goblen's *Insanity Isn't*. Both of these works pushed the aesthetic possibilities of Hip Hop in the context of theatre. Nicole Klaymoon's use of poetry, music, and movement gave insight into other dimensions of her characters' journey and to the flow of the storytelling. When she moved from a character to a movement section it heightened the energy and emotion. Her use of popping, boogaloo, and house dance forms were familiar and exciting but also were connected to the arch and intensified the state of chaos and conflict she invoked in the text. Her work about a woman's struggle with difference, "learning disabilities", and spirituality was deepened by its manifestation in the chaotic beauty and dynamic movements and driving beats of house music.

Rudi Goblen's piece *Insanity Isn't* directed by Teo Castellanos was a visual delight. The piece created a world of insanity, paranoia, and other worldly contact. Rudi transformed his B-Boy techniques into the realm of physical theatre/comedy. Rudi's rhymes are in the Hip Hop tradition of complex, abstract, and metaphorical language. At times I craved a more direct voice, or one that allowed for a greater range of emotional content. His character, an awkward and nerdy plebian dominated by his boss, was brought to life through tight movement and musical interaction. The music drove the work, creating tension and manifesting the dominance of the omnipotent boss. *Insanity Isn't* broke convention; the audience sat in a circle around the stage while Rudi moved thorough out the space creating a truly multi-dimensional experience.

remixing the ritual

hip hop commedia: facing the mask

Hip Hop Commedia is a project exploring the interaction between Hip Hop and Commedia dell'Arte conceived by Paul McIsaac and performed/created by Playback NYC. Our director Paul McIsaac writes.

> *In many ways the Commedia dell'Arte was the Hip Hop of its time. This bawdy irreverent improvised theatre that emerged from the popular festivals and market places of 15th century Italy came from the bottom up. As these rag tag traveling troupes spread among the lower classes of Renaissance Europe they became alternately adored by the upper classes or censored and banned. The characters, scenarios, masks, improvisation and comedy that emerged had its roots in Roman and Greek theatre and in earlier pre-literate "pagan" rites and storytelling.*
>
> *Archetypes like the Young Lovers, the Old Miser, the Pompous Doctor, the Scheming Servants and the vainglorious Braggart Soldier peopled these comic scenarios of greed, lust, revenge and forbidden love. And in time the Commedia was absorbed into the very heart of the Western theatre tradition from Shakespeare and Moliére, to Chaplin, the Marx Brothers, Monty Python, Seinfeld and Dave Chappelle. From Slapstick to the most sophisticated comedy of manners- our very sense of what's funny and how to make people laugh is rooted in this rich moment in the Renaissance.*
>
> *How does Hip Hop connect? Greed, lust, revenge and forbidden love are still part of the human condition... and Hip Hop. Braggarts, Schemers, Misers, Fakes and Lovers have different names and "masks" today but they are still with us and they are central themes for today's rappers. Hip Hop also has a rich and ancient heritage which we can trace back from its urban setting to*

> Black Poets, Jazz, Latin and Caribbean culture and through slavery to Mother Africa, the Griots and the same pre-literate "pagan" rites and storytelling as the Commedia.

In our Commedia project we are exploring the edges of our society, the mélange of isms that marginalize our communities. We do it through a comedic structure where no character is safe or above human desire and flaw. We explore the ability to play with all the archetypes to reveal a rich mix of our contradictions.

The development of this project was enhanced during Hip Hop Theater festival's development series *Critical Breaks*. We collaborated with Manchester's Benji Reid and Michael Fields, producing artistic director, of one of the foremost Commedia schools Dell' Arte. Benji's background as actor, director, popper, Hip Hopper and experience with physical theatre/comedy provided a bridge to the Commedia discipline and expertise of Michael Fields. Their collaboration gave us an inspiring one-two punch in developing staging, physicality, comedy, and character.

My Hip Hop persona has always been that of a conscious emcee who battles the evils of America through spirituality, skill, and love. I had not explored my flaws and contradictions. In *What You Say White Boy?* I amplified that personal mythology into my character B-Love who stands for love and battles ignorance but ultimately is "called out"on his White privilege. Hip Hop performers walk a line of assumed authenticity. The audience in a Hip Hop context would read my performance of content that is not critically engaging race as my actual view. In the theatre I can explore a character that is ignorant of racial issues and create a space for the audience to witness an important confrontation. If I am always the positive White Hip Hop artist who has all the right concerns it prevents a dynamic moment of recognition. *What You Say White Boy?* ends with a battle where the characters are broken down, revealing the layers of race, class, and gender. Each member of the company went through a similar process with the Commedia archetypes finding new homes in our contemporary world. Pantalone became Pops, Pulcinella- Poochie Brass Knuckles, The Zanies- Dj Inzane and Zane Child, Isabella- Queen Izaza, The Lovers- B-Love and Lady Plantium, and Capitano- Buck Grando. With these archetypes we used the modern scenario of the emcee battle.

The breakdown of the battle: Buck Grando, a Black middle class wanna be gangster rapper who is actually an NYU student steps to the mic in a variety of masks, from hard rock to a pimped out fool. He repeatedly gets dissed and sent packing. He finally takes the stage in a military jacket and delivers an impassioned speech on the problems of the poor. This speech moves to an  uplifting chant and quickly morphs into an Army recruiting rap. The other characters become hypnotized by the beat and B-Love is pushed to intervene. He steps forward and initiates an emcee battle where he calls out Buck Grando's lyrical impotence and malicious manipulation. He finishes off Grando with a verbal blast and climaxes with the statement "You are a traitor to your people!" This prompts Poochie Brass Knuckles, a bitter Black militant rapper who never got his shot, to come down from the sound booth and state "What you say White boy?" Poochie calls out B-Love's White privilege with sharp and cutting rhymes while B-Love counters with new agey and liberal rhetoric. Poochie escalates and ultimately says "you about as bitch as these females" This then prompts Queen Izaza, an over the top Afro-centric Spoken Word artist and Lady Platinum, a soul singer/waitress to put him and all the men in check.

hip hop theatre: space and place

Peter Brook's *The Empty Space* describes four types of theatre— Deadly Theatre, Holy Theatre, Rough Theatre, and Immediate Theatre. He has a strong critique of the deadening nature of much of theatre and its lack of real contact and entertainment. He talks about the maintenance of a status quo and a continual validation by the academy that legitimizes a very disconnected art practice.

Rough Theatre connects to both my work in Hip Hop and Commedia. Rough Theatre is often performed in non-traditional spaces, involves the audience, and plays at the edges of our social dynamics. If Hip Hop began in parks and community centers away from the commercialism of Broadway and mainstream music venues what can be said for Hip Hop now? It has been transformed and extracted into its rap form and found root in Corporate America.

Hip Hop's unique and vital energy is born from its roughness, its independence from the standard venue and its direct link to its community. Hip Hop, birthed in the seventies by Black and Latino youth, was a collective creation with people constantly sharing innovations in dance moves, lyrical flair, music, and fashion styles. Paul Carter Harrison writes "An opportunity for performative expression can be located in the daily rituals of life, including sporting events and in circuses, in storytelling and in public events, in clothing and hairstyles."[23]

Early Hip Hop forms were not initially presented or supported by either the academic institutions or the corporate world. Hip Hop's cultural force has been extracted and manipulated in various trend driven marketing periods. In the early eighties breaking or "breakdancing" found its way into television and films such as *Flashdance* and the *Breakin* movies.

---

[23] Harrison, Paul Carter "Praise/Word" *Black Theatre: Ritual Performance in the African Diaspora* Ed. Harrison, Paul Carter, Victor Leo Walker, and Gus II. Edwards.. Philadelphia: Temple University Press, 2002. p. 8.

Breaking then fell out of favor and was pronounced a dead fad by mainstream media. All over the world hardcore B-Boys and B-Girls kept the form alive and constantly evolving. There is a tension between the grassroots artistic and cultural development of Hip Hop and its commercial role. As Hip Hop becomes more and more mainstream and corporate, new forms and movements of Hip Hop are continually born.

One of these forms is Hip Hop Theatre. What are the motivations and the inspirations for this move? There is a surprisingly conservative approach in much of American Hip Hop Theatre. Hip Hop Theatre often takes its cues not from radical Black and multi-racial theatre traditions but rather from musical comedy, Shakespeare and very traditional relationships in playmaking and audience dynamic. In America I see a collision between Hip Hop Theatre's connection to a Black Theatre tradition and its rise as a multi-cultural platform striving for validation and support in twenty-first century America.

> ...Alain Locke's challenge to artists of the 1920's Harlem Renaissance, when he argued that Black dramatic art must be liberated not only from external disparagement but from its self imposed limitations by breaking away from established dramatic conventions to establish its own. Though emerging from a context of oppression, the ideal expressive products of Black Theatre throughout the Diaspora should reflect an alternative style of work or practice that is culturally specific and not limited to Western dramaturgical conventions. [24]

In the intersection of form, content, and venue we find the ingredients for innovative and culturally specific work. Can Hip Hop Theatre transform a proscenium theatre and allow for Hip Hop's raw, direct and ritualistic energy to manifest? Can a Hip Hop Theatre piece allow the audience to sit passively? What of the political choices of the Black Arts Movement, creating venues with local accessibility and connection to a specific community? How do the established forms of musical theatre and Shakespeare potentially limit the aesthetic growth of Hip Hop Theatre? When an artistic impulse or movement becomes institutionalized does it lose its significance? In Alain Locke's challenge I resonate with the push to deconstruct and transform an art practice with vigilance and integrity.

---

[24] Harrison, Paul Carter "Praise/Word" *Black Theatre: Ritual Performance in the African Diaspora* Ed. Harrison, Paul Carter, Victor Leo Walker, and Gus II. Edwards.. Philadelphia: Temple University Press, 2002. p. 4.

I have not yet seen a full Hip Hop Street Theatre production, or Hip Hop Theatre taking place in front of a protest, or site-specific locations like a steel mill or a shopping mall. I also repeatedly see Hip Hop Theatre opening in downtown venues, with high ticket prices, and often large White audiences. The Hip Hop Theater Festival has battled this with successful outreach to communities of color and youth groups. The theatre initiative of the New York City Parks Foundation has also given opportunity for such projects as Full Circle, Hip Hop Commedia, and Universes to connect to more public and diverse audiences.

Many of these restrictions are based in economics. In the Hip Hop Theatre world my generation of artists have a clear desire to be sustainable and break the starving artist mold. This is essential but has its effect on artistic and practical choices in terms of content, venue, and direction. In my own efforts to produce work I find that a major part of the conversation comes down to money and fundraising to make a project possible. I see this as linked to race, class, and time period. In the sixties art was deeply connected to a pervasive social justice movement that demanded rigorous political accountability.

In my work with Playback NYC we struggle with these questions. I would love to just rehearse non-stop and perform in trains, and on street corners, and who knows where else. As a younger artist I did just that; it is just not possible as an adult living in New York to build projects without income. That said, as we fundraise and secure money, I want to stay in a conversation about where we take our theatre and how we can continue to expand the theatrical impulse and wrestle with convention.

I'm a part of a collective with Kid Lucky called Beatboxer Entertainment. We have thrown free public subway parties where beatboxers, emcees, dancers, vocalists and poets jam on the NYC subway. During one party we collaborated with the Hip Hop Theater Festival and brought Playback NYC to a train station. It was a great moment of connecting theatre and public space.

Playback NYC had talked about bringing our Hip Hop Commedia work into nightclubs rather than theatres. *What You Say White Boy?* is set in a club. In the interactive and raucous environment of the nightclub we could break down audience and performer conventions. Part of our dream is to get the piece to the point where the characters are so strong that they are where they are. Whatever the venue, that's where there characters would exist and play.

In preparation for a Hip Hop Commedia performance in the fall of 2006 at Montclair University we discussed moving the setting of the show from an imagined club to the college venue. In that model we would, in the Commedia tradition, incorporate local politics, drama, and gossip from the college into the content of the piece. I struggled with the choice to either create in the context of the campus or to bring the control of a fictional club. Which choice allows more freedom for the audience? Which is more relevant? Which is predictable?

The dirt of Rough Theatre Peter Brook likens to the German electronic musicians who boasted the ability to produce any instrument better than the instrument itself. With analysis they discovered that the actual instruments contained breath and the texture of physical contact. He sees this dirt as applied to theatre as the immediacy of props, sets, and buckets becoming instruments. He writes

> *Of course, it is most of all dirt that gives the roughness its edge; filth and vulgarity are natural, obscenity is joyous: with these the spectacle takes on its socially liberating role, for by nature the popular theatre is anti-authoritarian, anti-traditional, anti-pomp, anti-pretense. This is the theatre of noise, and the theatre of noise is the theatre of applause.*[25]

This speaks to our Commedia performance; it plays in the dirt and the edge and there finds liberation. The dirt of sampled vinyl is marker of an authentic and non-commercial Hip Hop sound.

In 2006, we did a run of Hip Hop Commedia at the Bowery Poetry Club. Here the performance broke new ground. Instead of creating the theatrical illusion of an open mic we brought the show to a poetry club. We used the structure of the open mic to house our characters. We had hosts, soundmen, featured performers, a waitress, a bouncer, and a club owner all in character creating the atmosphere.

---

[25] Brook, Peter. *The Empty Space*. 1st American ed. New York: Atheneum, 1968. p. 68.

We began the night with traditional Commedia characters that then morphed into it their modern forms. The action moved from the stage and into the audience. The piece took the established feeling of a New York open mic and allowed it to move into a place of conscious theatrical exploration.

We performed *What You Say White Boy?* at Herbert Von King Park in Brooklyn on July 26th, 2006. Here the performance came to life. We structured the piece as a public show in a park with a special guest– "The Man." We wanted to play with the dominant White older male character (in Commedia Pantalone) that carries all the rank of race, gender, and class. The performance began with Poochie and B-Love taking the stage to warm up the crowd. Then Paul as "The Man" entered the park in a Black tuxedo accompanied by two bodyguards. It was amazing to watch the audience try to shake his hand and generally treat him as someone important though he was just an actor. That was an interesting tension in this performance– the line between performance and reality. The whole performance rode that edge, when Buck Grando– the wanna be hard rock came on the open mic– he was booed and even had things thrown at him.

Was the audience playing along with a theatrical performance or did they believe he was a real wanna be rapper? It was hard to tell. After the battle, which I described earlier, we as a multi-racial/gender community took on "The Man" and defeated him, which was a release for the audience and for us.

hip hop theatre: aesthetic articulation

Does Hip Hop Theatre need to make use of one of the elements of Hip Hop defined as emceeing, DJing, graffiti, dance (breaking, popping and locking), and beatboxing? Or is it enough that Hip Hop Theatre is made for and by the Hip Hop generation in relation to content and context?

In order for Hip Hop Theatre to push and expand theatrical form it must integrate its cultural and performance language into the structure of its theatre. In order for Hip Hop Theatre to innovate and transcend traditional or even radical theatre forms it must make use of its aesthetic traditions. I have felt this echoed by other artists who come from a Hip Hop cultural background and are still active in the Hip Hop scene.

Rickerby Hinds is a playwright from California who's written Hip Hop Theatre since 1989. In his plays Rickerby consciously chooses to work with Hip Hop's elements. He uses the choice of a Hip Hop element as a creative layer in his process. In his play *Dreamscape* about the murder of a young Black woman by a cop in Riverside, California, Rickerby casts the role of the officer and the coroner as a DJ. The DJ does not rock the party instead his role is transformed. He cuts and scratches audio samples to reconstruct Rickerby's text. The play becomes a battle between the humanity of the young woman and the bullets that killed her, described in technical details by the DJ coroner. The playful and endearing character of the young woman is contrasted by the embodiment of each wound in battle with this ominous and life stealing language. Rekirby's choices are exciting and pushing the possibilities of the form.

Kwikstep and La Roka, founders of Full Circle Productions are two important examples of Hip Hop artists who have brought their work into the theatre. They are both legends as breakers and also bring their poetry, monologues, song, and percussion to the stage. Their choreography transforms the B-Boy style into a theatrical tool. Breaking, which usually takes the form of exhibition and battle, takes on new meaning in their work. Their piece *Frontline* uses breaking and popping to invoke the intensity, discipline and horror of war. The piece *She's Gone* uses popping to evoke the loss of a woman whose partner was slain. The female character's duet with her lover's ghost creates a mournful beauty. Kwikstep is the first B-Boy I have seen to step forward and break the tough persona to reveal a vulnerable monologue. In Kwikstep and La Roka I see two artists who bring a wealth of Hip Hop skill and a commitment to expanding its use. Kwikstep says

> *There is a difference between Hip Hop being a used as an instrument and Hip Hop being instrumental to the Hip Hop artist. Hip Hop orchestrates by using one or all of its elements to tell its stories. Make sure you're well versed in the classic techniques of Hip Hop so that its aesthetic can be recognized. Hip Hop has four main elements, like the four wheels of a car, if you are lost on the many roads to Hip Hop, pull over and ask an experienced driver for directions.*"[26]

At the same time I recognize the passionate views of other integral Hip Hop Theatre artists such as Kamilah Forbes and Danny Hoch. Kamilah Forbes offers, "First and foremost I think its energy beyond the aesthetic. There's the "four elements," but what's even more important are the relevant issues to the Hip Hop culture and the Hip Hop generation."[27]

Kamilah asserts that it is the relevant issues that are of greatest importance. On one hand I agree with her and feel that the content and themes of many theatrical works are not connected to the issues facing the Hip Hop generation. What are these issues? Racism, sexism, capitalism, militarization, the prison industry, mass media, and grass roots resistance and creativity in the form of Hip Hop. These themes are relevant to many people not just the Hip Hop generation. Is it the language in which they are presented, the locality of the voice that they are presented with, and the context that the stories and performances are placed? Danny Hoch contributes

> *…All of the language, references, locales, contexts, and story reflected the dilemma of the Hip Hop generation; it didn't need any of the four elements of Hip Hop to qualify as a Hip Hop generation play…. On the other hand, a play titled Bomb-itty of*

---

[26] Phone interview with Kwikstep on November 19, 2007.
[27] Forbes, Kamilah "From the Dope Spot to Broadway" *Total Chaos: The Art and Aesthetics of Hip-Hop*. Ed. Chang, Jeff. New York: BasicCivitas Books, 2006. p. 80.

> *Errors was performed in New York City a few years a go...I found it painful to watch-not because it was poorly written, poorly acted, or poorly directed. It was actually a genius adaptation of Comedy of Errors.... But as universally and timeless as Shakespeare is, performing his plays in rap does two very damaging things. First, it sends the message that the Hip Hop generation has no important stories of its own, and for Hip Hop to qualify as theatre it must attach itself to such certified texts as those of Shakespeare. Secondly, it devalues hip-hop as art by relegating rap to humorous accompaniment. The feeling that results is of watching a Hip Hop minstrel show.*[28]

Here Danny Hoch comments on *Manchild Dilemma* that was criticized for not having any Hip Hop elements and contrasts it with *Bomb-itty of Errors*. His point is compelling and makes me want to open up my perspective. I agree whole heartedly with him that simply adding raps to what Danny Hoch calls "certified" texts does not move us towards creating a viable Hip Hop Theatre aesthetic or movement. At the same time if plays that don't utilize Hip Hop's creative elements are labeled as Hip Hop Theatre we may stunt the experimentation of the established complex aesthetics of Hip Hop into the theatrical language. I worry that seasoned playwrights will write plays from a Hip Hop "perspective" and they will be presented in a traditional theatrical form. How do the emcees, DJs, graffiti artists, beatboxers, breakers and poppers find their way into the theatre? Is there a way for collaboration? Are these distinctions necessary? Eisa Davis, playwright and Hip Hop head asserts

> *There's no way to essentialize all these artists work. Each recreates the genre as s/he creates individual pieces. Some are more interested in innovative theatrical form, utilizing one or more of the elements for storytelling and form, and others are interested in innovative narrative, making use of the sensibility, language, and stories of the Hip Hop generation for content Found in translation:*[29]

Eisa Davis introduces a voice that layers these desires. She does not place them in a hierarchy and therefore they are not at odds with each other. I hope that this statement produces dialogue, then collaboration and ultimately innovative Hip Hop Theatre. Hip Hop Theatre presenting original

---

[28] Hoch, Danny "Towards a Hip Hop Aesthetic" *Total Chaos: The Art and Aesthetics of Hip-Hop*.Ed. Chang, Jeff. New York: BasicCivitas Books, 2006. p. 358.

[29] Davis, Eisa "The Emergence of Hip Hop Theater" *Total Chaos: The Art and Aesthetics of Hip-Hop*.Ed. Chang, Jeff. New York: BasicCivitas Books, 2006. p.72.

and relevant stories, characters, and issues of our generations as well as integrating the elements of Hip Hop. I am not a purist in the sense of desiring that every Hip Hop Theatre piece be presented with rapped verse, be backed by a DJ or have a graffiti backdrop. In fact I am not into the idea of entire works in verse. In my solo piece *Boom Bap Meditations* I consciously chose to not write rhymes for each character. I don't want the hot dog salesman rapping. That's not his rhythm or language. I want to honor the voice he represents in the context of my New York City life. I am finding the ways that beatboxing, freestyle and popping integrates into my storytelling and into themes that I find relevant to my generation. It is a synergy of these two sides that will ultimately create a vital Hip Hop Theatre. As long as they are at odds we will be limited in content and form. Eisa continues:

> *He talked about the two major Epochs in drama: The theatre of articulate and the theatre of the inarticulate…Hip Hop joins the articulate with the inarticulate. The lyrics provide the articulation of the intellect, the need to speak plainly or with complexity, with irony, with local and personal specificity, satire, longing- and the beat brings the inarticulate release of pure music, of the drum, of our primal rhythm. And we can flip it. The lyrics can be inarticulate, the pure feeling evoked by a curse word, a nonsense rhyme- and the music can be intellectual not danceable, just something to contemplate, to analyze. When Hip Hop moves from the corner and into a theatre, you get the one-two punch. Articulate-inarticulateness. Restoring Theatre to its full power.*[30]

Here Eisa Davis articulates with great clarity the power of Hip Hop's heightened forms of lyricism and music to create a theatre that fuses traditions and remixes separated form. This is an essential aspect of the Hip Hop aesthetic– the ability to fuse, remix, and layer. I remember hearing Grandmaster Flash talk about how Hip Hop could break musical rules and bring samples from multiple genres, in different keys, and make a track that worked. Hip Hop's rule is that it has no rules except the elusive funk of its final product. The process of getting to that funk is alchemical and requires a rebellious experimentation and intuitive improvisation. An essential element of Hip Hop is its counterpoint to established art institu-

---

[30] Davis, Eisa "The Emergence of Hip Hop Theater" *Total Chaos: The Art and Aesthetics of Hip-Hop.* Ed. Chang, Jeff. New York: BasicCivitas Books, 2006. p. 73.

tions. It must have a force that mixes discipline with rebellion. Hip Hop is also a reclamation of ritual. It is not a bourgeois passive experience but a tradition rooted in community.

> *The number one thing that makes what we do Hip Hop theatre is the ritual and community interaction. We understand the audience is socially, spiritually, and intellectually implicated in what goes on. So when I bust Word Becomes Flesh in Seattle in front of a bunch of managerial old White ladies that are on the board of directors, they don't understand what is going on and they don't give me anything back then that affects the collective energy in the room. So the same three hundred silver-haired ladies in Seattle if by the end of Word becomes Flesh, they have moved to a place where they feel empowered to vocalize how they're doing then the ritual has worked...that's what makes it Hip Hop-because the cipher continues to move.*[31]

In my solo work if the audience is not ready to respond to my call, play with my characters, interact and maybe even get on stage, it's going to be a tough night. Part of my skill as an emcee, Playback conductor and educator is learning how to facilitate an active and responsive audience. For me, this will always be a vital part of Hip Hop Theatre.

Hip Hop Theatre is the marrying of Hip Hop's artistic language with the storytelling of the theatre. It is expanding the interdisciplinary nature of performance to include the tools of freestyle, emceeing, DJing, Hip Hop dance, and the visual language of graffiti. As Danny Hoch alluded to this is not enough. It is also using these elements and tools to tell stories that are vital, current and relevant to the Hip Hop generation. When a beat maker samples an old vinyl record they transform the soul of that sound into something new. If we are going to reference classic text or ancient myth we should apply that transformation. At the same time Hip Hop's elements should and will be transformed. A DJ's scratching won't just be for exhibition of skill but now could create a rhythm and texture to support an actor's gesture; a movement of anxiety and tension. A beatboxer could use their sounds to support a poetic monologue and become part of the emotional language. At *Process 06*, a Hip Hop Theatre work-

---

[31] Joseph Bamuthi, Marc "From the Dope Spot to Broadway" *Total Chaos: The Art and Aesthetics of Hip-Hop*.Ed. Chang, Jeff. New York: BasicCivitas Books, 2006. p. 81.

shop festival in Manchester, England director Karena Johnson explored using Hip Hop's elements with her participants in just such a way. They presented a piece that told the story of a love triangle between a man and a woman and another woman. Rather than dialogue they used the language of popping and turntablism to create the mood, character, and conflict of the story.

Creating a Hip Hop aesthetic in the realm of theatre is about expanding and transforming the foundations of the two converging worlds and disciplines. I also hope that it will be a collaboration of seasoned Hip Hop artists, theatre and performance artists, and those who bridge the worlds.

hip hop★s aesthetic voice

Looking at a Hip Hop aesthetic, a lot of the writing and discussion has been by cultural critics and artists who are influenced by Hip Hop or used to do Hip Hop. I define a Hip Hop artist as someone who actively practice and performs one or more of the elements of Hip Hop in relation to a community of peers. I want to delve into the thoughts and writings of primary Hip Hop artists, pioneers and innovators. I want to weave their thoughts and philosophies into context with those other voices and move closer to articulating the Hip Hop aesthetic. In conversation with my Goddard MFA advisor Jackie Hayes, she asked me why Hip Hop? Why do I stay with it? Reading *The Wu Tang Manual* by RZA, a legendary producer, emcee, martial artist, philosopher and entrepreneur reminded me of why. It is my culture. It is my primary artistic influence and school. It is the artistic expression and culture that I have spent the last twenty years following, practicing, discussing, critiquing, and engaging in.

Even in its current commercialization there is so much that remains unexplored, marginalized, and untapped. I want to be part of pushing and challenging its manifestation, scholarship and artistic expansion. I recognize the challenges of the hyper commercialization and its limiting and oppressive forces. I also realize I am in this for the long haul. Just as Jazz has gone through many transformations, there are still artists pushing and reinventing its form while also honoring its past. There is a force, a creative impulse, and a cultural history that will always draw me to Hip Hop.

RZA states

> *In the beginning I had no true understanding of how music works-theory, harmony, chords…traditionally structured…. In a way this was one of those times where a lack of knowledge was power, because there wasn't anything in the way of what I wanted to express. I just took sounds that sounded good to my ear and put them together*[32]

32 RZA Norris, Chris. *The Wu-Tang Manual*. 1st Riverhead trade pbk. ed. New York: Riverhead Books, 2005. p. 204.

There is a rebellious and anarchistic force to Hip Hop that I love. It is science fiction, the rebel forces transforming the empire's tools. It is free of classical tradition, conservatory training and rules. Hip Hop producers approached music through instinct, intuition and combined musical elements in ways no one had.

> *My instinct was keep it sparse. The sparseness leaves more ideas for the mind. If you notice, when you get a very complex piece of music, your mind tends to follow the music. When you have a sparse piece of music, your mind imagines its own things about the music. It fills in the blank...Music only needs a pulse.... It makes order out of noise.*[33]

Hip Hop musical production is often sparse and full of space and texture. In the space there is room for the lyrics to take center stage. The music becomes more of a textural, cinematic and emotional support for the poetry and storytelling. There are "schools" in Hip Hop production that are more pop oriented in form. I am looking at the producers who made tracks that were closer to films or theatre pieces. I see this musical aesthetic of sampling, space and unconventional layering of music, film dialogue, noises and environmental sounds as a key Hip Hop aesthetic. I am interested in how this aesthetic applies to performance and staged work.

> *In a way running a live Hip Hop show is like DJ'ing a party. In fact before every show, our DJ comes up to me and asks, "What do you want to do? And I look at the crowd and say, "You know what, lets set em up like this"-you know DJ style.*[34]

RZA talks about the lack of rehearsal in preparing for their shows. He affirms that it is in the improvisation and the crowd interaction that the show is born. For many Hip Hop artists their artistic practice is not a role that they train for or rehearse. It is part of their daily lives, expression and social interaction. Unlike an actor whose connection to a part begins with a script: for Hip Hop artists their rhymes, art, dance and music are daily personal, social and professional practices. I write rhymes and make beats that may never make it the stage or recorded medium but they are part of

---

[33] RZA Norris, Chris. *The Wu-Tang Manual*. 1st Riverhead trade pbk. ed. New York: Riverhead Books, 2005. p. 204.

[34] RZA Norris, Chris. *The Wu-Tang Manual*. 1st Riverhead trade pbk. ed. New York: Riverhead Books, 2005. P. 206

my continual exploration. I spit freestyles that manifest only in the social context of a party, a street cypher, or even a private moment of expression. Yet they still contribute to my ability and skill to create performed and recorded public work.

The community orientated nature of call and response and the rebellious and spontaneous nature of improvisation are essential elements of Hip Hop. The DJ is the storyteller, their venue the party. In the unpredictable environment of a party the DJ creates the structure that holds it all together. That balance of skill and chaos is part of the Hip Hop aesthetic.

> *The Question, then, remains much as it does in the study of the heavens, whether Hip Hop is, in fact, a closed universe-bound to re-collapse, ultimately, in a fire ball akin to its birth- or an open one, destined to expand forever, until its cold, dark, and dead.*[35]

This question by media assassin Harry Allen touches back to my conversations with peers about the future of Hip Hop and ultimately my own involvement in this cultural form. The answer is not binary but layered. The key is to find the balance between honoring the past and encouraging an expansive and rich development of Hip Hop. Longtime B-Boy and groundbreaking visual artist Doze writes:

> *Yes hip-hop is a part of my life. I become more full and more powerful going forward, not staying still and just reaping the benefits of what I did twenty-five years ago. I know a lot of b-boys, they just sit around and do that all day.... What I am saying is that I went through what my idea of Hip Hop is, I passed the torch to those that have lived their experiences through Hip Hop.... It's always been communication to me, and it's always been a more benevolent society, a more helping, more community based kinda thing. Where everybody sticks together and looks out for each other and talks about new ideas...*[36]

Doze illuminates the collective nature of Hip Hop. It is first and foremost a gathering, a cipher, a group of graff artists exchanging black books[37],

---

[35] Allen, Harry "Dreams of a Final Theory" *Total Chaos: The Art and Aesthetics of Hip-Hop*.Ed. Chang, Jeff. New York: BasicCivitas Books, 2006. p. 9.

[36] Codes and The B-boy Stigmata interview with Doze Ed. Chang, Jeff. *Total Chaos: The Art and Aesthetics of Hip-Hop*. New York: BasicCivitas Books, 2006. p. 326.

[37] The traditional sketch books that graffiti artists use to practice and sketch their pieces. The Black Book is also used for exchanging tags and pieces.

DJs practicing their cuts. It always balances the individual development of expression with a collective moment of contact and collaboration. In that social ritual are the seeds for a process that encourages group building and mutual desire for improvement. In Manchester, England I saw first hand the collective and public nature of Hip Hop. When I was at Process 06 I talked about a freestyle event that took place on Mondays in NYC and folks started up their own freestyle Monday. It started with four people and now has grown to an event that attracts thirty to forty people who build their improvisational skills through a series of freestyle exercises.

> *The communal spirit animates the full spectrum of these rituals and performances, including black Baptist church ceremonies, rhythm & blues music, and the black arts movement in the United States; canboulay rituals and calypso drama in Trinidad, carnival and condoble in Brazil; rituals of the Omo peoples in the lower Omo River valley in southwest Ethiopia; the planting rites ceremony of the Bedik peoples in Senegal; Yoruba Masquerades and the ritual dramas of Wole Soyinka in Nigeria.... Most black African in the Diaspora who create performative rituals do so to reaffirm the life force of the community by engaging the community in an experience that reinforces the collective worldview in which the natural rhythms and cosmic balances of the community, despite periodic disruptions, are in harmony.*[38]

This communal spirit attracts me to Hip Hop. From my experiences at Rock Steady anniversaries, Hip Hop shows, and the Subway Series this public and collective energy is inspiring. The danger is that when Hip Hop's cultural forms interact with the corruptive nature of capitalism, racism, sexism, and homophobia its benevolence becomes distorted and we get gangster rap, homophobic lyrics and sexist videos. Interestingly enough the Manchester freestyle Mondays instituted guidelines challenging its participants to stay away from racist, sexist, and homophobic content. This raises another challenge– the delicate line between censorship and the facilitation of safe and non-oppressive space.

---

[38] Harrison, Paul Carter, Victor Leo Walker, and Gus II. Edwards. *Black Theatre: Ritual Performance in the African Diaspora*. Philadelphia: Temple University Press, 2002. p. 14.

hip hop theatre: concerns, contradictions and limitations?

One of my concerns is that "Hip Hop Theatre" is already being used as a marketing tag and a way to attract audiences. There are artists who use this tag expressly for the purpose of securing funding and getting exposure without an established Hip Hop practice. I am disturbed that so early in the creative genesis of this Hip Hop Theatre movement it already faces these contradictions. I naively had hoped that Hip Hop Theatre would be a sanctuary from the market driven metamorphosis of Hip Hop music.

My other concern is one consistently highlighted by the group Universes who have purposely stayed away from the term Hip Hop Theatre. Universes' experience, skill set, and perspective are shaped by Hip Hop and they incorporate beatboxing and vocal sampling in their work; they do not want to be trapped by the word Hip Hop. In creating Hip Hop Theatre can we create a space where the Hip Hop generation finds reflection, connection, and representation. Or are we creating a box to limit our possibilities around form and expression?

As a White man there are contradictions that I must keep mindful of and face in my participation in Hip Hop. For the most part my experience has been positive and supported and the moments of confrontation have been essential in the development of a critical race analysis. My concerns around privilege contribute to a hesitance to take a central role in this process of creating a new aesthetic. At the same time I feel that I have come too far and invested too much to shy away from my role in the Hip Hop Theatre community as well as Hip Hop culture in general. I will just have to stay open and committed to being in dialogue with both supportive and challenging voices.

hip hop theatre: the future of the remix

The use of poetry and movement in theatre as a meta form that reaches into the unconscious, dreams, and primal and emotional territories is vital in my opinion to creating theatre. The use of specifically Hip Hop and related forms such as house, drum 'n bass, and Spoken Word to create a new contemporary aesthetic; that for me is Hip Hop Theatre. An artist could use modern dance, Jazz, or another poetic form to add that layer. Hip Hop Theatre allows for the Hip Hop generations to integrate the rich and diverse languages of Hip Hop to tell stories in new ways. The continuum of theatre as a vital human ritual for negotiating the complexities of our experiences is made richer and more inclusive by the making of Hip Hop Theatre.

I sit with hope for Hip Hop Theatre, dreaming of stages alight with insight and poetic rigor. I await tales of reflection and works that challenge and surprise me. I crave a ritual to process the maddening nature of our world. I have seen and felt the genius of our Hip Hop Generation. I also see the traps and pitfalls snaring our creative expansion. It is my sincere hope that Hip Hop Theatre will provide a space for innovation, for a greater diversity in theatre making, and give a new venue for Hip Hop's culture and language.

boom bap meditations: reflections on the process

My father, Steve Ben Israel, has done solo performance since I can remember. As a kid I was amazed and delighted watching him tell stories, transform into characters, change his voice, and move with blinding speed between each piece. It was magic and I was in on the secrets. My home was the rehearsal studio and laboratory where he would try out his bits on my mother and I. He is still doing it. Growing up with this interaction planted a seed in me, a seed to explore that magic for myself. Like many sons, it has been a tentative journey to step into my father's form.

My own history of performance begins in youth ensemble theatre but as a young adult shifted to Spoken Word and then to Hip Hop (emceeing, producing and beatboxing). I later found myself moving through experimental improvisational ensembles, bands, and theatre groups. I stayed away from the solo zone. Inside I knew that there was a creative desire and voice that I needed to explore and manifest. This desire along with some economic shifts pushed me to towards creating my first solo performance *Boom Bap Meditations.*

This chapter will present the script, explore the process of creating the work and reflect on work in progress performances. My hope is that this document will provide insight to fellow solo-performers both new and experienced. It is also my hope that it might provide clues for other Hip Hop and Spoken Word artists who are moving into the realm of theatre. For the veterans of solo performance and specifically Hip Hop Theatre I hope that it might affirm, remind, and raise questions in their established practice.

script: boom bap meditations

Sound Cues in Bold Italic

*Enter beatboxing in a private moment
come to center*

Baba

This is for street heads and beat heads
Not for those who speak dread but for those who squash beef not meat heads…

Step out into Aussie Hip Hopper- " in the pub, holding it down, down under."

Not weak feds who defeats free speech or cops who beat heads
This is for teachers who work on weekends

Step out into Teacher- "Welcome to the assembly quiet down for the show."

Not for cats who rhyme till the beats ends but for emcees with rhyme etiquette
Who never get the props they deserve
For wordsmiths with the nerve to transcend the urge to merge with the simplistic gimmick scourge

Step out into Junita- "I write rhymes with my teacher, Baba…"

Feel the surge of some real Hip Hop verve from Planet Earth NYC to specific!

Drop Rimshot beat

Say New York City! Say New York City!

Baba

I grew up in New York City! We got any New York heads in the house? I remember when I was five years old and I would make tapes with my pops. He asked me "What do you want to be when you grow up?"

Conversation between Father and son, embodying young Baba

Young Baba

I want to be a super hero!

Pops

What are you gonna do?

Young Baba

Fight the Bad Guys

Pops

Do you know who the bad guys are?

Young Baba

Yeah! Galactus, Sabretooth, Megatron!

Pops

Well, son, the real bad guys are in Washington DC, in the White House, you know Ronald Reagan, Capitalism, the money system, racism, what's happening in South America

Baba

Well he was right, and I kept thinking about what he said, and I was looking for something, something that was fun, and also had a message. I found Hip Hop!

Say New York City! Say New York City!

> **Slow down beat w/ filter**

Move away from audience body language slows and demonstrates fear

Say Orange Alert

Say What's in your bag?

> **Bass textures**

terrified

                                            I am terrified of AIDS

rappers with attitudes
                those who kill DJs

I am terrified of Bush and a push to war
I am terrified of those I love, not having health care
I am terrified of **me** not having health care

> **Cut filtered drums Bass line in unison with I am terrified**

Moving from up center to down center and delivering lines directly to audience

I am terrified of cops who stare at kids with fear in their eyes
instead of protection

I am terrified of teachers who scream
and count the hours to the bell

I am terrified of those who think teachers and schools
don't deserve priority over war

I am terrified of a news system that keeps us
locked in   terror

I am terrified of guns and nervous hands
and humiliated spirits

I am terrified of a music industry with no conscience
I am terrified of military recruiters who see poor youth as potential property

I am terrified of White, Black and Latino kids who diss Arab kids with the power of their words

I am too terrified to worry about
terrorism
Chant Snippet Transition

Transform into meditative Tai Chi movements into spin and pop up with rhythmic popping finish into frozen statute then break...

Baba

Now Living in New York City you can make some very unique friends. One of my unique friends is Akim the Funk Buddha. That's right that's really his name.

Akim came from Zimbabwe, From Africa, and he came to New York City to create and perform.

Akim would perform on street corners (*beatbox*)
On the subway Beep Boop watch the closing doors Beep Boop watching your closing mind
And when Akim was hungry he would perform in Falafel restaurants (*beatbox* hummus *scratch* taboulie)

New Age Music

And when Akim was fed he would perform in new age centers and Ashrams
Then after he had meditated he would perform at raves

Beatboxing with house movement and "move your body" vocal sample)

Add bassline

Raver

Hey man can I have some Acid?

Akim

I don't do acid, I use oxygen

Oxygen dance into hands moving towards stillness

Baba

What Akim really taught me about was stillness. The way he did this was through freeze posing. Now if you don't know what freeze posing is, that's when you paint yourself and turn into a human statue. Now Akim would paint himself gold and I would paint myself silver and together we were two of New York City's finest street performers.

("Ching" Move "Ching" Move "Ching" Move)

Sound Effect

We only moved when someone gave us money, it was very practical street performance.

Now one night we were coming back from street performing, Akim was gold and I was silver. My face, neck, my arms were all silver, except the palms of my hands.

We were hungry and going to get a bagel. We were in the Village, the only place you can be gold and silver and going to get a bagel and its all good.

Now we were about to get the bagel when all of a sudden I hear "Akim!"

W. African Drumming

Akim's Friend

Akim its good to see you brother, its always good to see a brother from the motherland. I needed to see you, I have been having a hard time Akim, I have been stressed, pressure about to pop I mean these White motherfuckers, these White devil motherfuckers have been driving me crazy. My boss has been riding me, Landlord on my back, I mean my boss is White, my landlord is White, my mayor is White, my governor is White, my president is White, my motherfucking dishes are White. These White devils they control it all, can you feel me brother?

Baba

Oh shit! He didn't realize that under this silver I was one of those White devils

Akim's Friend

Akim be vigilant there are White devils all around us! Peace Akim and peace brother

Baba

White shadow
Concealed in silver
Black breath burned with truth
Underneath this silver, I felt like maybe he was right, maybe us White motherfuckers are the problem, and here was I hearing words I wasn't supposed to hear. I thought I would never see him again and then there he was standing in front of McDonalds.

Akim hold my bagel. So I walked towards him held out my hand and showed him my palm and said "I am still your brother"

White appropriation medley

We hear a medley of Elvis, The Rolling Stones, Vanilla ICE, Eminem answered by Public Enemy and Mos Def

Black Music background loop

Black Music

this is the music that originates
in African landscapes
now broadcast on mix tapes
I got the privilege to be a part of this culture

respect this

This is Black music

I am a guest at best blessed to express stress over beats with finesse

Elvis was a tragic star that fell so far from what music meant
pimped by his management
the cross over sex appeal
let's get real
                      rock and roll

was a code for soul
to get R&B played on White radio
its not long hair and guitars
that came later
       The British invader

singing the Blues without paying dues
this country is infused with African philosophy
this music is African property and should be respected properly

      the transcendental state of Blackness
I want to have this
but to think its mine is madness
to bear the bounce but not the burden
all I can posses is the presence of mind
not to be blind
and look beyond the curtain
what's on the stage?
unfair wage and prison cage?
racist policy human mockery
a militant monopoly that absorbs culture into a commodity

so White kids let's not make the same mistake, musical rape
respect build trust in order to integrate
know our privilege is power unchecked at the gate

I have felt alone in a world that is cold
found peace and strength in stories told
Hip Hop molds my flow language and soul
so to this I owe humility
yeah I'm nice on the mic
my spirit would recite poetic transmissions whether Black or White
these words were given form and function
through African diction and tradition
as I find my way is this contradiction?
should I hang up the mic and seek somewhere else

I know Hip Hop   like I know myself

I remember coming up
pumping X-Clan

like I can't be a White man
used to get love from my Black fam
it was like I wanted to change who I was
measure myself by the thickness of my blood
and the depth of my love

always stepped with sincerity
got love from the crowd staring at me
it was a spiritual calling
that I could not refuse
this path I had to choose it
but let's not forget this is   Black music

Bar Sound Atmosphere

Aussie Hip Hopper

Music you want to talk about fuckin' music mate, how about some Aussie Hip Hop. Fuck all this American Hip Hop they've lost the plot its all bling bling and strip clubs mate. Over here mate we keep bloody Hip Hop alive Aussie Hip Hop mate! Four elements mate, who knows em? You don't even know the elements of Hip Hop! Come on name em that's right graffiti you from Australia. That's right Aussie Hip Hop the DJ that's where it all starts when's the last time you saw a DJ in an American video?

Fuckin Aussy Hip Hop Scratch

Senior

My names is Beatrice, now when I first heard there was going to be a Hip Hop workshop at the seniors center I got a bit nervous. But then this sweet young man walked with a big smile and he started making these amazing sounds with his mouth. It was just magical. Then he asked me to do it.

Beatrice Beatboxes

Missy Track "Toys"

Junita

My name is Junita and I have this poetry teacher named Baba and he be working with me on poetry and metaphors and alliteration. You know what alliteration is. I am not going to tell you. And he encourages me to write from my heart and I do cause I got a lot of love in my heart. I got a lot of love for the ladies. Cause I am a lady who loves the ladies. Thats how I get down. And I be writing love poetry. And you know when I am in my neighborhood I get looks but I hang in the Village cause that's where I can be me. I don't just write love poetry I battle too. You wanna hear me spit?

You want to test me I don't think so
My names Junita respect my flow
Hit you with a pillow smack you with a dildo

And Baba be like "you should expand your lyrical horizons"

The Roots

Bro

Dude man bro dude bro dude man bro bro dude man bro
Dude you missed it bro I like went to the show and The Roots were rocking live.
That's right the Roots but dude there was this bro he was like the opening act,
and his name was Baba and he had a red beard man bro just like mine and I was super high
off the killer dank skunk and bro he started freestyling and beatboxing and then he pulled out a fucking didgeridoo like from the Aborigines man, here in Massachusetts. Bro you fucking missed it (*pause*)
Dude I just had like a flash back. Dude he was like droning and droning then started making a beat through the didge and it was like drone beat drone beat droneeee

Motown

DawN's Father

Now when I first heard my daughter DawN was going to marry a young man named Baba who was a rapper I got very excited because I was going to have me a strong (*pause*) proud (*pause*) **Black** son-in-law. But when I met the motherfucker, he looked like Grizzly Adams. So I took a breath invited him in the car, we talked, I listened, and we connected and that boy can beatbox his ass off!

Beatbox

You are good with the beatbox mate! I heard you're mums from Australia! Ah, you know you are then mate! Yeah thats right, Aussie Hip Hop! Now what really gets me pissed, these Aussies rapping with American accentsDon't let me catch you rapping in an American accent you're not from G-Unit your from Gymea. You know I want to go down to the pub have a few with me mates, get a bit pissed and have some fun. What is with the underground Hip Hop in America– its too serious to fucking political who is the Mumia Abu Jamal anyway? I never heard him rap mate. I think these fuckin Americans have lost its all about Aussie Hip Hop. You know what I am sick of hearing about Black Americans and their problems I just want to do fucking Hip Hop!

Flute Poem w/ live bass

Bass Beat for the freestyle

Freestyle: Improvisation

I.S. 5 Teacher

Ok so you are ready, great, ok I.S. 5 I would like to introduce Rap Connections, oh I am sorry Hip Hop Connections. Now I.S. 5 you have been good this year so we brought you this special assembly show. Now it's a Hip Hop show but don't make any noise! Jenny do you need to leave now? Peter, put that book under the seat! Before the show I have a few announcements. First of all there were students who were cutting school yesterday and one of them got hit by a car. That's right. Is this funny? Look it was scary and I did not know if he was going to make it. Do you remember last year during parent teacher conferences there was a parent who was killed crossing the boulevard, you know what we call that Boulevard, The Boulevard of Death and now let's give it up for Hip Hop Connections!

Baba

Ok… well I am Baba from Hip Hop Connections! This is a Hip Hop show, we are going to talk and answer questions but you will also have to make some noise. Let me hear you! and I would like talk to you about beatboxing. I need a volunteer from the audience.

Beatbox lesson with volunteer

Survivor track: sound cue on "Drop that beat!"

Say Hip Hop!

Say Hip Hop!

Drop Atmospheric Park Sounds

Hot Dog Salesman

Hot dog, hot dog! That's what I do, I sell hot dogs, I have been doing it a long time. I got a stand in Washington Square Park, you know in Greenwich Village. I mean I seen it all here. The people, wow, there's every kind of person in this park. You got your punk rockers, your hippity hoppers, your street performers, your acrobats, your sword swallowers, your dealers, your NYU students, your folks singers, and hey if they buy a hot dog they're ok with me. So one day, and it's a beautiful day, this big guy comes over to me. I mean a big guy. He orders three hotdogs. One with mustard, one with relish, and one with both. 1 2 3- boom cool. I give em the hot dogs he gives me the money. Then he looks at me and he says I owe him a dollar. Now I know my business. I do the math. And wait a second he owes me a dollar. He tells me I better give me a dollar or else. Now he doesn't know, but I used to be a boxer. I mean I am older, I got a family, I breathe but then he says something about my mother, I am about to whack him when all of a sudden this hippy guy comes over to me and he's like "I'm the money fairy, I'm the money fairy," he gives one dollar to me and one to the big guy. Hey honestly I cracked up and everything was cool.

Cut sounds

Baba

That hippy guy with the long hair, that was my father. I was about six years old and that was a scary moment but my dad turned into the money fairy gave each of those guys a dollar. He would tell me that sometimes you get a chance to test your art on the anvil of life.

Subtle bassline

Now my father is from Brooklyn and my mother is from Australia. I don't know if you know much about Australia but it has a similar history to America, a history of oppression and violence against the indigenous community. That history still plays out today.

I lived in Australia for three years, and in Sydney there was one neighborhood that had the edge and intensity of parts of New York, was Redfern. Living in New York I developed a special radar, spider sense, I knew when to cross the street, duck into a dinner, or jump in a cab. Now Redfern is the area where the indigenous community known as the Koori live. Redfern is near, Chinatown, Surry Hills an artsy and gentrifying (becoming White) neighborhood, and it also next to Central Station where all these communities meet and sometimes collide.

One day I was coming up from Central Station and I felt it. There were two Koori girls checking out two White Aussie girls who were on the phone.

Drop Atmospheric Park Sounds

Aussie Girl

Singing riff- I am on the phone

Baba

The two Koori girls were asking for cigarettes

Koori Girls

Cigarette cigarette!

Aussie Girl

I am on the phone, all alone, in my own zone, (maybe if I ignore them they will go away?)

Koori Girls

Cigarette cigarette!

These girls in my neighborhood, on my land and they won't even look at me.

Cut sounds
Baba

It was about to go down. One of the Koori girls reached down and picked up a broken glass bottle

Beatbox

The White girls were like "who is this crazy White guy with the beard?"
The Koori girls were like "who is this crazy White guy with the beard?"
The White girls took off and I was left standing with the two Koori girls.
They looked at me and said "Can you do that again?"

Beatbox

Then we talked about music and they told me their favorite artist was Mariah Carey

Scratch in Mariah Acapella

Jam

We talked about their neighborhood, the problems in their neighborhood, and the brand new community center and how excited they were about it.
Gone were the cigarettes and gone was the broken glass bottle
And what was left was…

Beatbox outro

building blocks: the path to boom bap meditations

contact theatre manchester, england 2005

In 2005, Benji Reid, a veteran and visionary Hip Hop Theatre artist, invited me to perform with my father at Contact Theatre in Manchester, England. This performance was the beginning of my transition from Hip Hop/Spoken Word solo performance to creating a solo theatrical work. At this phase I had collected stories that I wanted to bring to the stage but was telling them in narrator form. I had not yet developed characters, staging, and the overall arch.

notes preceding contact theatre show november 2005

This was my work in progress set list for Contact Theatre in Manchester. I never finalize my set list till I am physically in the venue. As a performer I want to interact with local issues, language, and context.

Contact Theatre set list December 2005
A cappella freestyle into a beat 2-3 mins- set the stage for who I am. freestyle about the trip, my initial experience of Manchester, shout outs- drop beat, create hip hop mood.
Tell me your story 3mins- fade out into NYC chant!
NYC- 3 mins acapella- Lyric about NYC, establish where I am from set mood for next piece. End with call and response "say NYC, NYC"
Changes 3min This track reflects on the change as a universal constant through two narratives"
Akim story 4 mins- ends with "*I am still your brother*" transition into questioning "am I your brother?" **Black Music 2 mins**
Flute 2 mins- sample and loop flute- Signal through the flamesh
Beatbox 3 mins
"Beatbox saves the day" 3mins see scripted version
Terrified 1 min
Recruit 2-3 mins then moves into Hip Hop set.
Emergency 4 / Survivor 4

reflections on works in progress performances: 2005-2007

The following is a collection of process journals about the creation of *Boom Bap Meditations*. I have grouped excerpts in relation to themes, questions, and structure. I present this after the script so that you, the reader, will gain insight into the choices I have made. The process journals reflect my personal process as well as notes from a variety of work in progress performances. These performances have been critical to the development of the show. I am an artist whose performance is linked to the moment and to direct audience interaction. The work in progress performances took place before and after two weeks of rehearsal with my director Morganics. The rehearsal process was instrumental in refining and redefining initial ideas with the all important outside eye of the director. My recent work in progress performance at the *Critical Breaks Development Series* on Oct. 13th 2007, presented by the Hip Hop Theater Festival was the first collaboration with musician/DJ Yako 440. Yako is a multi-instrumentalist and my collaborator in Hip Hop music and Playback NYC. Yako and I rehearsed for three days with outside input from Paul McIsaac and Mtume Gant.

how do i develop a solo show? 2005-2007

How do I work on the structure of the show? I want to develop sound cues and transitions between poems, stories, and raps. I want to use existing material but also create new text. How can I give shape to the overall piece and work on the individual moments at the same time? I have started to script a collection of autobiographical stories. I shared one of the stories at my MFA residency at Goddard College. After receiving feedback, I decided I would leave room for riffing and freestyle in my storytelling. I want to develop discipline and clarity in relation to structure, pacing, blocking, and physicality.

Well it's been hard for me to get into a studio and create by myself. I am not sure if that is because of time or also because it is so foreign to my process. My work has always been in relation to audience or ensemble. Whether it has been street performance, Hip Hop clubs, Playback Theatre, or Commedia; the art has come out of interaction. My solo process is non traditional. I do rehearse but it tends to be when I share my stories at dinner parties, on the subway, at a restaurant, waiting for a movie to start, moments alone, with friends, and even with strangers.

what is the essence of this show? what do i bring to the table?

In creating this solo work I want to experiment and break new ground. I also want to solidify and affirm my craft as an emcee, beatboxer, poet, and music producer. I want to push my acting and reveal my storytelling. This piece is rooted in the themes of improvisation as lifestyle. It is also about my father as artistic improviser in everyday life and a personal inspiration. The cultural and physical landscape of New York is important. I want an audience who has never been to New York to experience it and for people from New York City to feel "that's my home." I also want to touch on my mother and her birthplace, Australia. I want to represent the power of improvisation, of freestyle, to create moments of humanity. I want to share moments that break down walls, stop and shift violence, transform space and make magic.

the white savior

My time at Goddard College was an important part of my process. At our residencies I presented excerpts of my stories. The feedback I received at Goddard has been great and it was a supportive environment to develop the work. The following is a reflection on feedback from Lisa Wolpe, a Goddard MFA-IA graduate and founder/artistic director of the Los Angeles Women's Shakespeare Company.

Lisa voiced concern about my stories reinforcing the White savior. How do I communicate my genuine moments of intervention and creative possibility without reproducing the White savior? It makes me think of all the times when I had a long beard and got called Jesus– I would always counter with "hey didn't you know Jesus was Black"– this flipped the script. Race is another essential theme to this work. I want to find a way to bring my critical research on race to the stage. My journey as a White man in Hip Hop and negotiating my relationship to Black culture is a definite theme. I want to connect race in Australia the parallels and intersections America.

Lisa also encouraged me to develop the characters– I am nervous about that– for one character performance is new for me. Do I want to create a naturalistic or realistic dramatic space. In my Playback experience we strive for metaphor and when playing other people we do not characterize but stand in the role of a given character. Playback works with real stories and people; there is the challenge of improvising a caricature, as opposed to creating a character with specific body language, accent, and content.

lack of voice: deepening the characters

At Goddard I shared a story where I encountered a moment of violence between four young women, two Koori[39] and two White Australian. In the story, *Beatbox saves the day*, I intervene with a beatbox and end up having a conversation and jam with the Koori youth. I received feedback about the lack of voice for the Koori youth in the story. I must also mention that in the actual experience I was with my partner Steph–I, who is a woman of color, and was also an essential part of that intervention. I have not found a way to bring her into the performance.

I think my hesitation in developing the Koori voice is based on not wanting to caricaturize the Koori young women. I am thinking about stepping out and speaking from their inner voice "These White girls in our neighborhood, these White girls on our land" This phrase layers the levels of adolescent territorialism and the deeper layer of colonialism, imperialism, and genocide.

What would my body do in this moment? I am also hearing a beat coming in under the phrases. I wonder about the potential of using audio clips of Koori girls. Morganics who will direct the piece works with Koori youth all the time. Could it be more powerful to go into a freeze and hear a Koori girl's voice expressing her feelings in this area? This also highlights a creative tension between pushing my own voice and using technology to support.

In continuing to share *beatbox saves the day* I am affirmed in its effectiveness. I have a greater feel for the rhythm of the story. I am trimming the fat and finding the essential lines and moments. When I am moving into the Koori girls I am starting to use a simple accent now in the midst of the threatening words of "cigarette cigarette" I step forward and state "these girls in my neighborhood these girls on my land and they won't even look at me." I added the second line because it speaks to the White fear that makes communities of color invisible. The White girls have become more musical which for me is about the obliviousness of privilege. The inno-

---

39 Koori refers to the indigenous Australian community in New South Wales.

cence of a little melodic riff is also about ignoring the harsh history and reality around you. It also contrasts the beatbox, which is about breaking through and direct communication.

new world theater: intersections conference april 2006

Here are reflections on my performance at New WORLD Theater: New WORLD Theater has been an integral part of my development as an artist. I took excerpts of my stories to the Intersections Conference at New WORLD Theater. I had a limited amount of time so I chose two of the stories *beatbox saves the day* and the piece *I am still your brother*.

notes after the new world theater performance: bring the complexities of race to the stage

In the story, *I am still your brother* I am painted silver, mistaken for Black and then reveal my Whiteness with the phrase "I am still your brother." I then go into a poem called *Black Music*. This handles the positive but problematic concluding moment of *I am still your brother*. I really like the assertion of a human connection that transcends race. I feel in my heart the truth of that moment but I also feel that it oversimplifies the conversation on race. There are essential differences in the experience of people of different races in this country and in the world. I don't want my piece to simply say, "we are all one and we should all get along." It is my desire to create work that takes on a layered approach to negotiating race. *Black Music* is a is a self-examination of being a White artist in Black music and raises questions around privilege.

improvisation vs. structure

Reading back on these notes I am reminded of an essential question, which has come up in rehearsal and in talkbacks. Do I stick verbatim to the script? I remember during an earlier feedback session at Goddard there was affirmation of the need to maintain a balance of structure and spontaneity in the storytelling. Doing so allows for the work to not only share my perspective and predetermined expression but also allows for potential interaction with local culture, language, audience, and artists. Jonathan Fox, founder of Playback Theatre writes about the improvisational nature of storytelling "There is a positive side to this inevitable variation from one telling to the next. Slight additions or deletions accrue from one telling to another enrich, improve, and add to the power of the tale."[40]

When I performed *Boom Bap Meditations* in the UK, I did a freestyle using local Manchester slang, which really connected me to the audience. The more I write about this the more I feel that this is an essential element of my work. I don't want to create static work that cannot respond to the moment. One of the biggest differences between my performance at Podium Mozaeik[41] in Amsterdam and the 245 Live[42] performance in Brooklyn was the spirit of improvisation. The first time did the show I stuck to the timing and text that Morganics, my director, and I had set. Morganics stressed the importance of this. His concern was that improvisation could make the piece drag. It was important for me to work at the level of discipline. I am also worried about losing spontaneity. I want to find a balance with this. I don't want to be undisciplined, indulgent, or extraneous. I do feel that something is lost if I do not have moments built in when I can play with the specific time, place and audience.

humor

I was excited when I performed an excerpt of *Boom Bap Meditations* for around seventy teenagers at Brooklyn Academy of Music Cafe. I was curious how they would react. I had never done the show for this audience. In the past my work has been political and introspective but now I am also making people laugh. I am starting to gain more confidence that will allow me to stretch further.

Humor is at the heart of my father's work. I have always admired his ability to communicate serious political and personal content while making people laugh. My experience with *Boom Bap Meditations* has given me the chance to do this as well. There is joy and release in creating a space for humor.

---

[40] Fox, Jonathan. *Acts of Service: Spontaneity, Commitment, Tradition in the Nonscripted Theatre.* New Paltz, NY: Tusitala Publishing 1994. p. 14.
[41] Work in progress performance at Podium Mozaiek in Amsterdam April 19th 2007.
[42] 245 Live performance May 2006- This is the space where I rehearsed with director Morganics and presented the first full performance of *Boom Bap Meditations*.

reflections on the process: moving towards collaboration with director morganics spring 2006

In my desire to research *Boom Bap Meditations* I went to see a solo performance *Recollections* by Kendra Ware that combined influences of Butoh, performance art, and music from RZA of the Wu Tang Clan. The piece used very little text and focused on movement, primal sound, voice, and sound collage. The work was so different from my current aesthetic. This was refreshing and also challenging. It made me both inspired to broaden my style and also intimidated by such an emotional, vulnerable, and physical performance. It really made me think about how I might find moments of physical exploration as transitions in my stories. Right now I think my work is somewhere between emcee, poet, storyteller, and comedian. *Recollections* was in a whole other zone of abstract and emotional terrain. It had almost no text and the emotion was communicated through physicality, music, melody and interaction with the space. The stage was filled with torn up and discarded newspapers, creating the feeling of a homeless person at the edge of our city life.

In my work what would it mean to go from a poem/rap to a soundscape accompanied by subtle or visceral movement? How can I open myself to that? What if after *I am still your brother*– instead of going into a piece with words I went into a soundscape and movement that explored the contradictions around brotherhood and race?

the role of music

My work is greatly influenced by music and specifically the musical aesthetics of Hip Hop. This might be the literal inclusion of beatboxing or rhymes but it also applies to the pacing and feel of the actual work. At the finish of the story *beatbox saves the day*, I end with the line "gone were the cigarettes, gone was the bottle and what was left was… After replacing the word "music" with a melodic beatbox I am now thinking about what it might mean to have a sound cue. Will I collaborate with Yako for live music accompaniment? I don't want to hide behind sound cues but I do want to produce and work with soundscapes.

Yako accompanied me in my performance at the Hip Hop Theater Festival's Critical Breaks Development Series. It felt great and I am excited to see how his role will develop. I do feel that he was able to add new layers of sound and allow for live interaction in the sound cues. We received feedback that suggested we look into his stage positioning. In many Hip Hop Theatre shows the DJ/musician is placed stationary either stage right or left. What might it mean to have multiple stations with Yako playing different instruments or triggering sounds from multiple positions?

process journal: creation of boom bap meditations in collaboration with morganics

We began our process with a series of brainstorming exercises. Morganics had me make a brain tree of words I associate with my identity and sense of self. We free-associated and built lists and connections. It was interesting to look at how themes and thru lines emerged that connected the pieces and overall direction of the show.

integration of movement

Morganics had me develop a movement language. We focused on movement that broke the shape of the emcee. We played with levels, with floor work, with rolls and spins. As we developed this vocabulary we then experimented with integrating character and text. This helped to break open the transition between characters and stories.

clarity of lines and moving through space

How to do I move past the spoken word/comedian style of being on stage- the style of just standing center or ambling about?

I needed help with articulating how I moved on stage. Morganics helped to ensure that I used the whole space and that I moved with intention. It was amazing the simple details that I had not considered. For example when I would reference another character in a story being consistent with where I placed my gaze. This was challenging for me but as I worked at it, it helped me to focus and feel grounded in the pieces. I started to feel a sense of where each character lived and where their space was. We also played with finding key gestures for characters and stories that articulated a moment. These gestures became motifs throughout the piece.

contrast of character

Initially was anxious about doing characters. It has become my favorite part, finding their rhythm and voice. The ability to step out of my voice is my attraction to theatre. We worked on the physicality of each character– having certain restrictions– not using hands with an exaggerated head movement or hands on hips. These guidelines helped me to move from beat to beat.

taking my time

Morganics had two main mantras- slow down and don't overpower everything. I am so used to hyping the crowd that I was doing every piece at maximum volume and intensity. Morganics really worked with me to find other tempos and volumes. In an effort to break up my text heavy performance we decided to pre-record two of my poems. I then set music to the poems and we worked on adding movement.

race

Morganics and I addressed the transition between the *I am still your brother* story and the poem *Black Music*. We developed a movement piece to a musical mix of Elvis, Rolling Stones, Vanilla Ice and Eminem. The music climaxes with Public Enemy and Mos Def calling these White cultural legends into question in the context of Blackness and authenticity. It allows me to explore these contradictions in my body and move to a different channel in relation to the storytelling. This mix helps to set a context for the *Black Music* poem

character challenges

I am still your brother transitions into the White appropriation mix and then it's broken by *Black Music*, which then breaks into a Aussie Hip Hopper. That was a rhythm that we started to find and ride. Create a vibe then shift and break it. At first I was really intimidated by doing the Aussie character. I struggled with getting into the harshness of his voice and was challenged by the accent, yet he is vital to the show. The Aussie Hip Hopper provides a counter point to the resolve of *I am still your brother* and *Black Music*.

Maxwell Golden, a Hip Hop Theatre peer, came over from London to see my Amsterdam performance of *Boom Bap Meditations*. He really pushed me to do the Aussie Hip Hopper. I had pretty much decided I wasn't going to do that piece. I am glad Maxwell pushed me to keep the Aussie character because he really adds an important dynamic to the show. He brings another culture and international layer. The Aussie Hip Hopper is proud of his Aussie Hip Hop and hyper critical of American commercial rap music. His critique of American Hip Hop/rap is on point but then it twists and reveals a layer of racism and his dissociation with the Blackness of Hip Hop. He adds the element of aggression and represents a contradiction of Whiteness, the ability to use Black culture and at the same time dismiss it. When I lived in Australia I encountered the attitude of dissing American Hip Hop by accomplished White Aussie Hip Hoppers who extracted the skills, style, and passion of old school Hip Hop culture from its Black context.

shifting the voice: finding other tellers

All of my stories were told from my perspective. Morganics suggested doing the *money fairy story* from the perspective of the hot dog salesman. This worked great, it allowed me to once again break out of my primary flow and inhabit another voice.

boom bap meditations:
work in progress performance may 2006 at 245 live

Man I was nervous before the show, really nervous. I have not been nervous before a show in years. It felt great to do the piece. I missed a few cues– revealing the palm of my hand earlier in the Akim piece and also leaving out the connection of Koori and Aboriginal. I am excited to carve out and find resources to make more time for this!

feedback from the 245 live show

Kid Lucky feedback– positive Whiteness– Kid Lucky felt that there should be more acknowledgement of the positive role of White Hip Hop artists and the way Hip Hop has connected people from different backgrounds. He felt this would create more of a balance.

DawN– Public Enemy concerns– DawN was concerned that the Chuck D lyrics wouldn't read to a general audience– how to address that?

David– transitions– David felt that I should work on other modes of transition from character to character.

One woman needed more clarity about Koori as a part of the Aboriginal community. This would be addressed by not forgetting that text.

process festival manchester, uk: breaking cycles summer august 2006

At the Process Festival in Manchester I performed along artists and groups Will Power, Karena Johnson, Robert Hilton, and *Life of a B-Boy* directed by Benji Reid. The event was a process focused Hip Hop Theatre workshop festival. Here I was in a community of peers and performed for a room full of Hip Hop Theatre artists, actors, emcees, dancers, DJs, and graffiti artists. It was a live and interactive audience. This was my best performance. The energy of the characters came to life, the audience received the stories, and I was able to connect the performance with the moment. I brought in slang and topics in my freestyle that were local and relevant to Manchester. I also had a spontaneous collaboration with a UK dancer. This was the only time I tried that.

amsterdam: podium mozaiek april 19th 2007 audience interaction

In Amsterdam I expanded the piece where I am performing in a Queens school. I played more with the audience and brought someone up from the audience and cast them as an eight year old from Queens. Then I taught them to beatbox. This was great! I really wanted to have a moment where I brought in the audience in a direct way. I love the tradition of audience interaction from Hip Hop to magicians to Theatre of the Oppressed. There are many different intentions but the key is challenging the passivity of the audience. The audience becomes empowered to add to the action. This allows for local voices, greater diversity of ideas, and the potential for a feeling of community and collectivity. The playful interaction in the show in Amsterdam and the way the audience got involved would not have happened if I had not brought a volunteer up. From my experience in Playback I know that a volunteer can become a voice for the collective group.

beginnings and endings

I have played with ending *Boom Bap Meditations* in different ways. I used to end with "gone were the cigarettes, gone was the bottle and all that was left was music." With help from DawN Crandell I dropped "music" and after "gone were the cigarettes, gone was the bottle and all that was left was" I do a melodic beatbox riff. It is stronger now that the piece ends embodying music.

When I first performed the *Boom Bap Meditations* the beginning was disconnected from the audience. By starting in the role of a storyteller and emcee I interact directly with the audience. This breaks the formality of the space, establishes the culture of Hip Hop. I don't desire or expect a passive audience. Its breaks the fourth wall from moment one. I can bring in something about the venue, the political climate, or the local culture.

Paul McIsaac offered that the beginning should signal the ritual and form of the journey. He appreciated the constant surprises of the show but felt that the beginning did not prepare the audience for the character work and storytelling that would follow. I had been starting with an a cappella rhyme called *This is for*. It is a strong lyric that has poetic power and establishes a direct voice. Paul suggested I weave some of the characters into this poem. We found breaks in the poem where I can then introduce two of the characters.

future

Morganics, Yako and I will rehearse September 2008. *Boom Bap Meditations* premiers at the Hip Hop Theater Festival in NYC October 2008.

For booking info@openthoughtmusic.com

multi-media/links

To view excerpts of *Boom Bap Meditations*

Link: http://www.me.com/gallery/#100044

Links:

Openthoughtmusic.com (Baba Israel and Yako website)

Subphonikmusic.com (Indie label with Core Rhythm)

Myspace.com/babaisraelandyako440

Myspace.com/subphonikforces

Morganics.info

Playbacknyc.com

Hiphopcommedia.com

Bamiphoto.com (*Boom Bap Meditations* photographer)

donnacat.com (*Remixing the Ritual* graphic designer)

Hip Hop Theater resources:

Hiphoptheaterfest.org

Breakingcycles.co.uk

bibliography

Artaud, Antonin. *The Theatre and its Double.* New York: Grove Press, 1958.

Brook, Peter. *The Empty Space.* 1st American ed. New York: Atheneum, 1968.

Bean, Annemarie. Hatch, James Vernon, and Brooks McNamara. *Inside the Minstrel Mask: Readings in Nineteenth-Century Blackface Minstrelsy.* Hanover, NH: Wesleyan University Press, 1996.

Brecht, Bertolt Willett, John, and Ed. and Tr. *Brecht on Theatre; the Development of an Aesthetic.* 1st ed. New York: Hill and Wang, 1964.

Bonney, Jo. *Extreme Exposure: An Anthology of Solo Performance Texts from the Twentieth Century.* 1st ed. New York: Theatre Communications Group, 2000.

Chang, Jeff. *Can't Stop, Won't Stop: A History of the Hip-Hop Generation.* 1st ed. New York: St. Martin's Press, 2005.

Chang, Jeff. *Total Chaos: The Art and Aesthetics of Hip-Hop.* New York: BasicCivitas Books, 2006.

Dolan, Jill. *Utopia in Performance: Finding Hope at the Theatre.* Ann Arbor: University of Michigan Press, 2005.

Dyson, Michael Eric. *The Michael Eric Dyson Reader.* New York: Basic Civitas Books, 2004.

Esslin, Martin. *Brecht: The Man and His Work.* New rev. ed. Garden City, N.Y: Anchor Books, 1971.

Fanon, Frantz. *The Wretched of the Earth. Uniform Title: Damnés De La Terre.* English. New York: Grove Press, 1965.

Ferguson, John. *Aristotle's Poetics.* New York: Hill and Wang, 1985.

bibliography

Fox, Jonathan. *Acts of Service: Spontaneity, Commitment, Tradition in the Nonscripted Theatre*. New Paltz, NY: Tusitala Publishing, 1994.

Graves, James Bau. *Cultural Democracy: The Arts, Community, and the Public Purpose*. Urbana: University of Illinois Press, 2005.

Harrison, Paul Carter, Victor Leo Walker, and Gus II. Edwards. *Black Theatre: Ritual Performance in the African Diaspora*. Philadelphia: Temple University Press, 2002.

Hill, Errol. *The Theatre of Black Americans: A Collection of Critical Essays*. Englewood Cliffs, N.J: Prentice-Hall, 1980.

hooks, bell. *Teaching to Transgress: Education as the Practice of Freedom*. New York: Routledge, 1994.

hooks, bell. *Outlaw Culture: Resisting Representations*. New York: Routledge, 1994.

Kitwana, Bakari. *Why White Kids Love Hip-Hop: Wankstas, Wiggers, Wannabes, and the New Reality of Race in America*. New York: Basic Civitas Books, 2005.

Matsuo, Basho, and Sam Hamill. *The Essential Basho*. 1st. ed. Boston: Shambhala, 1999.

Neal, Mark Anthony, and Murray Forman. *That's the Joint! The Hip-Hop Studies Reader*. New York: Routledge, 2004.

RZA Norris, Chris. *The Wu-Tang Manual*. 1st Riverhead trade pbk. ed. New York: Riverhead Books, 2005.

Schloss, Joseph Glenn. *Making Beats: The Art of Sample-Based Hip-Hop*. Middletown, Conn: Wesleyan University Press, 2004 p.29

Shange, Ntozake. *Three Pieces*. New York, N.Y: Penguin, 1982.

performances

Bamuthi Joseph, Marc. *Scourge*. Brooklyn, New York: Kumble Theatre June 8th 2007.

D, Jonzi. *Aeroplane Man*. Washington D.C.: Hip Hop Theatre Festival 2004.

Forbes, Kamilah. *Rhyme Deferred*. New York, New York: Nuyorican Poets Café, 1999. Hip Hop Theatre Festival 2001.

Goblen, Rudi *Insanity Isn't* Miami, Florida: Miami Light Box Studio, Miami Project Hip Hop, September 28, 2007.

Hinds, Rickerby *Dreamscape* New York, NY Critical Breaks Development Series: Abrons Arts Center October 2007.

Hoch, Danny *Till the Break of Dawn* New York, NY: Abrons Arts Center September 4th 2007.

Klaymoon, Nicole. *The Sixth Vowel*. Miami, Florida: Miami Light Box Studio, Miami Project Hip Hop, September 28, 2007.

Morganics *Crouching B-Boy, Hidden Dreadlocks* Ashalnd, Oregon: Oregon Shakespeare Festival October 2007.

Universes *Live from the Edge* Miami, Florida: Colony Theatre, Miami Project Hip Hop, September 29, 2007.

list of plates

p. 7 Playback NYC at Hip Hop Theatre Festival, San Francisco Yerba Buena Center for the Arts 2005 Photo by Clyde Valentin

p. 8 (top) Baba Israel at the Metro Club in Sydney Australia Photo: unknown

p. 8 (bottom) Baba Israel at the Subway Series 2006 Photo: unknown

p. 9 Baba Israel, DawN, and Yako at the Bardavon Theatre Poughkeepsie, NY March 2007 Photo by Kay Churchill

p. 10 Baba Israel performing *Boom Bap Meditations* at Critical Breaks Development Series presented by Hip Hop Theatre Festival October 2007 Photo by Bami Adedoyin

p. 11 (left) Pamela Mayo Israel at Theatre for the New City Photo: Ira Cohen

p. 11 (right) Steve Ben Israel at Anti-War protest New York, NY Photo: Yuko

p. 12 Nuclear mutant mask by Pamela Mayo Israel Photo: unknown

p. 15 Yako 440 performing *Boom Bap Meditations* Critical Breaks Development Series presented by Hip Hop Theatre Festival at Abrons Art Center NY, NY October 2007 Photo by Bami

p. 17 Baba Israel and Steve Ben Israel New York, NY 2005 Photo by Richard Greene

p. 18 *Hip Hop Connections* piece by Yako 440 Photo by Yako 440

p. 33 Playback NYC at Hip Hop Theatre Festival, San Francisco Yerba Buena Center for the Arts 2005 Photo by Clyde Valentin

p. 44 Baba Israel and David Gandy in *What you Say White Boy?* at Montclair University Photo by Clyde Valentin

p. 49 (top) Cast of *What you Say White Boy?* at Montclair University Photo by Clyde Valentin

p. 50 (bottom) Cast of *What you Say White Boy?* at Montclair University Photo by Clyde Valentin

p. 84 Yako 440 performing *Boom Bap Meditations* Critical Breaks Development Series presented by Hip Hop Theatre Festival at Abrons Art Center NY, NY October 2007 Photo by Bami

p. 85 Baba Israel performing *Boom Bap Meditations* at Critical Breaks Development Series presented by Hip Hop Theatre Festival at Abrons Art Center NY, NY October 2007 Photo by Bami

p. 86 Baba Israel performing *Boom Bap Meditations* at Critical Breaks Development Series presented by Hip Hop Theatre Festival at Abrons Art Center NY, NY October 2007 Photo by Bami

p. 87 Baba Israel performing *Boom Bap Meditations* at Critical Breaks Development Series presented by Hip Hop Theatre Festival at Abrons Art Center NY, NY October 2007 Photo by Bami

www.ingramcontent.com/pod-product-compliance
Lightning Source LLC
Chambersburg PA
CBHW021021090426
42738CB00007B/852